民世安在鴻選集 8

民世安在鴻選集 8 - 資料篇 -

초 판 1쇄 인쇄 2004. 10. 8.
초 판 1쇄 발행 2004. 10. 15.

엮은이   고려대학교박물관
펴낸이   김경희
펴낸곳   (주)지식산업사
주소   서울시 종로구 통의동 35-18
전화   (02)734-1978(대)
팩스   (02)720-7900

인터넷한글문패 지식산업사
인터넷영문문패 www.jisik.co.kr
전자우편 jsp@jisik.co.kr, jisikco@chollian.net

등록번호 1-363
등록날짜 1969. 5. 8.

ⓒ 고려대학교박물관, 2004
ISBN 89-423-2056-2 04910
ISBN 89-423-0001-4 (세트)

책값 20,000원

이 책을 읽고 문의하고자 하는 이는 지식산업사 전자우편으로 연락 바랍니다.

* 이 책은 민세안재홍기념사업회, 경기문화재단, 평택시의 지원을 받아 출간되었습니다.

民世安在鴻選集 8

― 資料篇 ―

高麗大學校博物館 編

지식산업사

자료편을 내면서

흔히 박물관 하면 희귀 문화재나 고가의 골동품을 수집 전시하는 곳으로 생각하기 쉽다. 오늘날 박물관은 전문화·특성화의 방향으로 나아가고 있으며 근현대사 관련 자료의 수집 정리도 박물관의 새로운 영역으로 주목받고 있다. 그런데 일제의 강점에 따른 주요 자료의 일본 유출과 제2차 세계대전 뒤 조선총독부의 자료 소각, 해방 뒤 정치적 혼란과 한국전쟁 등으로 현대사 관련 자료는 오히려 희귀하다고 말할 수 있다.

고려대학교 박물관은 우리나라 최초의 대학교 부설 박물관이며, 그 수장 자료 또한 선사 시대에서 근현대에 이르기까지 양적으로나 질적으로 대학박물관으로서는 최대 규모를 자랑한다. 특히 최근 고려대학교 박물관은 전근대 자료 중심이라는 고정관념을 깨고 일제의 강압 통치와 그에 대한 항일운동, 이어지는 분단과 군사독재 아래서 민족의 고뇌어린 실천과 민중들의 생활상을 생생하게 보여주는 근현대 자료를 체계적으로 수집해 새로운 영역을 개척하고 있다. 이미 민영환·유길준가(家)의 기증 자료만 해도 독자적인 박물관 건립이 가능할 정도이다. 여기에 민세 안재홍 선생의 유족이 귀중한 자료를 제공해 주어 해방 뒤 역사 자료 또한 새롭게 확충되고 있다. 민세 선생의 계승자라 불리기도 한 손진태 선생의 자료가 얼마 전에 고려대학교 박물관에 기증된 데 이어 민세 선생의 자료가 기증되니 이 또한 깊은 인연이 아닐 수 없다.

두루 알다시피 민세 안재홍(1891~1965) 선생은 일제강점시기 일제에 의해 9차례나 투옥되었던 국내 민족주의 계열의 대표적인 이론가이자 지도자의 한 사람이다. 그는 1920년대 후반기에 일제와 민족개량주의에 대항하여 비타협적인 민족주의 계열과 사회주의 계열의 공동전선체인 신간회를 결성하는 데 주도적인 역할을 하였다. 해방 이후에는 건국준비위원회 부위원장, 국민당 당수, 남조선과도입법의원, 민정장관 등을 역임하면서 중도우파 진영의 지도자로 활동하다가 한국전쟁 당시에 납북되었다.

이번에 고려대학교 박물관이 유족으로부터 기증 받은 민세 선생 자료는 다음 몇 가지 종류로 나눌 수 있다. 일제강점시기에서 해방 직후까지 민세 선생이 신문과 잡지에 발표한 글, 해방 뒤 정치 활동과 연관된 자료, 과도입법의원과 민정장관 재직 때의 미군정청 등과 관련한 공문·서한 등의 문서류와 각종 성명서·선언문·보고서·각서 등의 원본 자료, 민세 선생의 독서노트·기행문·기타 미발표 원고, 민세 선생과 관련된 각종 보도기사류 등이다.

이 자료들 가운데 미군정시기 민정장관 재직 전후 미군정청 등과 관련한 공문·서한 등의 문서류를 중심으로 별도의 자료집 성격으로 선집 제8권을 엮었다. 미군정시기 문서류가 현재 국내에 거의 남아있지 않다는 현실과 민세 선생이 해방 직후 정치적 혼란기와 미군정시기에 주요 위치에서 다양한 활동을 전개했다는 점을 감안해 보면 일상적 편지나 메모지 한 장이라도 그 자료적 가치는 매우 크다고 할 수 있다. 이 가운데에서도 민세 선생이 남조선과도입법의원, 민정장관을 역임하면서 미군정 당국과 주고받은 문서류와 1948년 2월 2일

유엔 한국임시위원단 제2분과위원회의 회의록 등은 희귀한 당시 원본 자료로서 주목할 만한 것들이다.

고려대학교 박물관은 안재홍 자료의 수장 전시에 머무르지 않고 해당 자료의 출판을 통해 《민세안재홍선집》을 《민세안재홍전집》으로 완성시키고 "조화와 중용의 민족주의자 안재홍"의 사상을 정리해, 또다시 불거지고 있는 국민의 이념적 갈등 해소와 우리 민족의 숙원인 통일을 향한 남북 화해협력에 주요한 사상적 자양분을 제공하고자 한다.

먼저 귀중한 자료를 기증해 주신 민세 선생의 유족 안영찬 님, 안혜초 님께 깊이 감사드린다. 그리고 이번 자료집 발간에 재정적으로 도움을 준 민세안재홍선생기념사업회, 경기문화재단, 평택시에 감사드린다. 자료의 정리 및 전산화에 도움을 준 박한용 선생님의 노고에도 감사한 마음을 전한다. 특히 어려운 여건 속에서 이 자료를 보존해 주시고 훌륭한 책으로 만들어 준 지식산업사 김경희 사장님께 감사의 인사를 드린다.

2004년 10월 5일

고려대학교 박물관장

최 광 식

1946년

1947년

1948년

1949년

1965년

연대 미상

1946년

■ **사진_** 1947년 12월 12일 군정청 앞. 남조선과도입법의원 개원 1주년 기념.

American Delegation
U.S. - Soviet Joint Commission
Seoul, Korea.

October 11, 1946.

MEMORANDUM TO: Military Government Personnel

     Mr. An Chai Hong, a member of the Coalition
Committee, is travelling from Seoul to Kwang Ju on
urgent political business.

     The military transportation which he is using
has been provided for the purpose by the order of the
Commanding General.

     It is requested that military installations
will aid Mr. An Chai Hong by providing fuel and
any assistance which may be necessary.

                         L. M. BERTSCH
                         2nd Lt.   CMP.

LMB:w

American Delegation
U.S.-SOVIET JOINT COMMISSION
Seoul, Korea.

October 11, 1946.

MEMORANDUM TO: Military Government Personnel
               of Cholla Namdo,
               Kwang Ju, Korea.

The bearer Mr, An Chai Hong is in Kwang Ju

on urgent political business on behalf of the

Coalition Committee.   This Committee is officially

cooperating with the Commanding General in preparatory

measures for the creation of the South Korea Legisla-

ture.

Any assistance that can be given to Mr. An Chai

Hong within the scope of your procedure will be

appreciated.

L.M. BERTSCH
2nd Lt. CMP

Major General Archbold V. Arnold,   October 31, 1946
H Q AGF, Fort Monroe, Virginia, USA

Dear General Arnold,

        I had planned to come back to Seoul from my trip
the day Your Excellency left Korea but an automobile
trouble at Kangnung detained me a day so that I could
not see you off to my great regret.
        I fully agree with your opinion regarding Korean
problem, as was reported here from Washington, that
the Korean problem cannot be solved by the power of
the commanding generals of the USA and USSR, that it
should be done by the governmentsoof the two countries.
        I told Your Excellency that it was a matter of
regret that you could not continue to work in Korea but
it was reasuring that you were going to work for Korea
in Washington.
        At this time when the UN conference is being held
in New York and many things of concern are taking place
here in Korea, I believe you, who are well versed with
Korean situation, will be a great help in the solution
of our problem by making the understanding of your
President and the Department of State more correct and
abundant.
        I believe Your Excellency and your politicians
know best that to put Korea in the Soviet sphere of
influence is a worse condition than the era of Japanese
Imperialism.
        Virtual disruption of the US Soviet Joint conference
and delay in the establishment of the provisional
government is impeding construction work and making the
intreagues of agitators to gain strength.
        Any further protraction of this state of affairs,
we should not overlook, will become cause of destruction.
Last of all I pray for the health of you and your family.
This is only a private letter.

                        I remain,
                            Yours cordially,

                            Ahn Chai Hong
                            President,
                        The Han Sung Ilbo,

HEADQUARTERS
UNITED STATES ARMY MILITARY GOVERNMENT IN KOREA
Office of the Military Governor
Seoul, Korea

6 December 1946

Mr. Ahn, Chai-hong

You are requested to report to the Office of the Secretary of the Korean Interim Legislative Assembly (Room 214, Capitol Building, Seoul) before noon on 10 December 1946.

A meeting of all the members of the Legislature will be called by the Secretary of the Korean Interim Legislative Assembly at 10:00 AM on 11 December in the Throne Room of the Capitol Building for the purpose of electing a Chairman.

The formal opening of the Legislature will take place at 12 noon, on 12 December 1946.

C. G. HELMICK
Brigadier General, United States Army
Acting Military Governor

變任書

日帝支配로부터解放된以來國民을爲한貴下의渡華한勢力에對하야敬意를表하는同時에現下朝鮮國民의政治的、社會的、經濟的改革發展에더욱貢獻케하기爲하야本官은西紀一千九百四十六年八月二十四日附法令第百十八號에依한權限으로써玆에貴下를前朝鮮過渡立法議院議員에選任하게되였음을無上의光榮으로生覺합니다

本議院의開院式은西紀一千九百四十六年十二月十二日立法議院議事堂에서擧行할豫定임니다

詳細한點은軍政長官으로부터各位에게通知할것입니다

議院議長

21

西紀一千九百四十六年十二月六日

駐朝鮮美國陸軍司令官

美國陸軍中將　쫀、얼、커

安在鴻

座下

朝鮮過渡立法議院召集及開院式公告

一、朝鮮過渡立法議院議員諸位는西紀一千九百四十六年十二月十日正午까지同議院事務總長室（軍政廳第二百十四號）에來參하실事

一、同議院의議長은同議院事務總長司會下에同年十二月十一日午前十時軍政廳王冠室（第一會議室）에서金議員參集하야選擧할事

一、同議院의開院式은同年十二月十二日正午에擧行함

西紀一千九百四十六年十二月六日

在朝鮮美國軍政長官代理

代將 써•지•췔미크

安在鴻座下

HEADQUARTERS XXIV CORPS
Office of the Commanding General
APO 235
SEOUL, KOREA

7 December 1946

Mr. Ahn, Chai-hong
Seoul, Korea

Dear Mr. Ahn:

In view of your distinguished services on behalf of
the Korean people since their liberation from Japanese rule
and in order that you may further aid in the political, social
and economic progress of the Korean people at this time, I
take great pleasure in appointing you a member of the Interim
Legislative Assembly of South Korea under the authority
vested in me by Ordinance 118 of 24 August 1946.

The first meeting of the Assembly is scheduled for
12 December 1946 at the national Capitol in Seoul. The
Military Governor will inform you separately of detailed
arrangements for the initial session.

Faithfully yours,

JOHN R. HODGE
Lieutenant General, U. S. Army
Commanding

1947년

■ **사진_** 1947년 2월 10일 군정청 광장. 민정장관 취임연설 모습.

HEADQUARTERS
UNITED STATES ARMY FORCES IN KOREA
APO 235

Mr. Ahn, Chai Hong
Editor, Hyun Dai Ilbo,
192-11 Ton Am
Seoul, Korea.

Dear Mr. Ahn:

Since it is the function of the United States Army Forces
in Korea to prepare the way for an independent Korean Government, it
has been my policy to turn over, as time passes, more and more Governmental duties and responsibilities to Korean officials. Only in this
way can a gradual transition be made from a military government, which
was necessary at the outset, to a government operated by the Korean
people themselves.

Consequently, from the day the American forces arrived in
Korea it has been my policy to transfer the responsibilities to Korean
officials as rapidly as circumstances would permit. The transition
was actually so gradual that often it went unnoticed, but steadily more
and more duties were being performed by the Koreans, and less by the
Americans. When General Lerch announced, on September 12, 1946, that
the Korean Directors of the National Departments or offices would for-
mally undertake supervision over these major segments of the National
Government, it was merely an acknowledgment that Korean officials were
adequately prepared to assume a larger measure of responsibility for the
administration of government in Korea.

I think the time has now come when a further step can be
taken in the Koreanization of the government. I believe a Korean Civil
Administrator should be appointed to coordinate the work of the several
departments and offices that are now supervised by Korean Directors.
General Lerch and I have had this in mind for some time, and we have
given very careful attention to the selection of a Korean Civil Administrator. We have agreed that you, Mr. Ahn, by reason of your training,
your experience, your judicious temperament, your record of unfailing
patriotism, and your intimate knowledge of Korean affairs, are uniquely
fitted to perform the duties of the Civil Administrator.

I know of no position in the Government of Korea where a true
patriot can be of greater service to Korea and to the Korean people.
You appreciate, as I do, that there are no easy solutions for the problems that confront us. One of the most difficult problems that we must
face is the selection of qualified Korean personnel for a great many

important posts in the Government of Korea. This is a matter which
can be handled better by a Korean than by an American. I am sure
you will agree that we cannot be too careful in the selection of personnel if we are to build up a government that will be able to cope
with our difficult tasks. You know, as I do, that we must find answers for the host of problems that confront us, that we must patiently
and conscientiously work out the solutions to our police problem,
our food problem, our problem of dealing with Japanese collaborators.
It is one thing to criticize or to condemn; that is easy to do. It is
something entirely different to find practical, realistic solutions to
these problems that confront us; this task is difficult. But we must
not falter just because the task is a hard one; indeed the very difficulty must be a challenge to our imagination and our devotion to duty.

        I am persuaded that you, Mr. Ahn, could be of very great
service to Korea as Civil Administrator, and I sincerely hope you will
be willing to accept this pivotally important position in the Korean
Government. If you are willing to serve in this capacity, please inform me and keep the matter confidential until after my nomination of
you has been submitted for approval to the Korean Interim Legislature.

                Sincerely yours,

                JOHN R. HODGE
        Lieutenant General, United States Army
                Commanding

※ 민정장관 취임을 제안하는 내용으로 보아 1947년 1월 무렵으로 추정된다. 이 자료는 《민세안재홍선집》
   제2권에 "민정장관 취임을 제의한 하지주한미군사령관의 공한"이란 이름으로 실려 있다.

○ 親愛하― ... 쓴。

謹啓 在鴻貴下는

獨立朝鮮政府에 (達)하고자 하는 것을 닭는 것이 朝鮮駐屯美軍의

職務이 옮기에、時間의 經過에 따라 政府義務 及 責任을

(漸次)移讓함이 本官의 政策이어씀니다

이러함으로써 最初에 必要로 軍政府에서 朝鮮

人自身에 運營하는 政府로 (漸次)移行하는 事情이 許可

그럼으로 美軍이 朝鮮에 到着한 그 날부터 그 事業은

하는限 (迅速)히 責任을 朝鮮人官吏에게 移讓

本官의 政策이였음니다 (事實)은 (大端)히 漸

進的이라는 것에 따라 그것이 않지 않는 것으로 밨었읍니다

本官의 政策이 않읍니다 移行之 事實 大

(看)々朝鮮人이 運營하는 任務를 增加하고

運營하는것은 減少하였읍니다 一九四七年九月十五日에

더지少將께이 朝鮮人 本廳 部課長이 正式으로 軍政廳

大都署를 管理하게되었고 發表を것은 卽 朝鮮人

官吏가 行政責任을 더많이 負担乞 準備가 完分히

되는것을 認定함에 不過한것이며

本官은 現 軍政府의 朝鮮化에 対하 一步 前進

這特期不到未計以다고

朝鮮人部長이 管理하고있는 各部課의 事務를

調整함은 朝鮮人民政長官을 任命하여되었고

朝鮮人民政長官의 選擇에는 細心의 註意

懇念하여 朝鮮人民政長官의 選擇

此음니다. 더지少將과 本官은 이体을

룰하였음니다

두리는 貴下의 訓練經驗, 愼重한 氣質, 不屈한

愛國의 記錄, 朝鮮事情에 対한 親密한 知識을 가보와

貴戰이가 民政長官의 職責 責務를 遂行하는데 가장 適任

이라고하는데 意見이 一致되었읍니다

朝鮮政府內에서 眞正한 愛國者가 朝鮮사람 朝鮮人民

에게 奉仕할수있는 地位를 本官은 밝지못함니 容易한 解決

우리가 當面한 問題에 対하여서는 本官도 貴下도

策은 없바는데 貴下도 本官과같이 아니시며

입니다 우리가 当面하여서 가장 困難한 問題의

하나는 政府內의 重要한 地位에 資格있는 人員

을 選任한것입니다 이것을 美國人員과 朝鮮人

이더 강 反撥할수있는일이나 우리의 困難한

問題를 担當할수있는 政府를 建設하려면 우리

4.

그 人員 選擇에 있어서 많은 注意를 하여도 注意가 適當할 수 없다는데 貴下도 이에 贊同할 수 없을것도 同意할 것이라고 믿읍니다 貴下도 아니싫이 우리는 우리가 當面하는 많은 問題에 解答을 發見하여야 하고 우리 警察問題、食糧問題、對日協力者 取扱問題 等의 解決은 忍耐性이있게 良心的으로 하지않으면 안되 것입니다 非難批判하는것은 容易한것이지만 되나 우리가 當面하는 이러한 問題의 實際的 現實的 解決策을 發見하는것은 (金錢)別問題입니다 그것은 困難한것입니다 그러나 이로서 難하다고 蹉跌버려서는 안되겠읍니다 도리어 이의 困難 性이 우리의 想像力가 義務에 對한 志誠心에

昭和　年　月　日

34

挑戰합니다

本官은 貴下가 民政長官으로 朝鮮에 赴任하며

大端히 크게 奉任하실수 있다고 榮覺합니다

貴下가 朝鮮政府에서 가장 重要한 이 地位를

依然 受諾하시기를 真心으로 希望합니다

貴下가 이 資格으로 奉仕하기를 快諾하신다면

本官에게 그뜻을 通報하여주고 貴下의 住命을

同意를 어더 議院에 通附한 대까지

此件은 秘密히 부치시기를 바랍니다

陸軍中將 一兒 R.

昭和　　年　　月　　日

Dear Lt. Leonard M. Bertsch,   3 Feb 1947

   1. There is at present factious rivalries in the Interim
     Legislature. If consent is sought by recommendation
     before the appointment of the Civil Administrator, there
     will be considerable opposition by intreagues. Then
     personal prestige may be impaired in case of failure.
     Therefore, we think it is better to appoint first and
     then ask for the confirmation and consent of the
     Legislature according to Section V of Ordinance 118
     which reads:

     "It shall also have the power (to review all past
     appointments to the Military Government above the
     Civil Service Status of Class 4 and) to confirm and
     assent consent to all such future aaapointments."

   2. If it takes time before appointment after the
     acceptance of the post by Mr. Ahn, the news may leak
     rumours spread and noise and obstruction may be caused
     we are afraid.Should such happen Mr. Ahn as well as
     the MG whuld be put in an unpleasant position. Therefore
     it is necessary that the appointmen and announcement be
     made as soon as possible.

   3. Mr. Ahn asks your assistance to have Dr. Kuisic Kimm
     attent the meeting when General Hodge meets Mr. Ahn
     with regard to this problem.

Mr. Lee Soong Pock, I and others assisting Mr. Ahn with
regard to this case are of opinion that the two points are
of exceeding importance, and so your assurance as to these
points is necessary before Mr. Ahn's acceptance of the
post.to prevent loss of face not only of Mr. Ahn alone
but also of Lr. General Hodge.

一、現在 立法議院 内部에는 臺灣의 對立이 있어 民政
　　官의 任命 以前에 推薦으로 同意를 求하고

　　한 諸署의 好意로써 이 個人의 威信上에

　　影響이 不美하게 되므로 軍政長官 第二……

　　므로 第二項에 그러한 未來의 任命을 追認

　　한 諸의 同意하는 權限이 있음 이의

　　追認으로 求하고 또 그 選擇이 要當하고 認함.

一、모 其 議하여 있음이 不話하고 世間에 請直이

　　雜音이 好 生하게 되면 軍隊 及 諸們이

　　이에 義하여 廣州……

　　다고 認함.

昭和　　年　　月　　日

一. 故○將軍이 會談 못해 州立 會員을
金博士로서 招待하여 大會談해서五때
正았다.

(알선)

Ordinance No. 118

Section V

It shall also have the power (to review all past appointments to the Military government above the Civil service Status of Class 4 and) to confirm and consent to all such future appointments.

※ 1947년 2월 3일 Bertsch 중위에게 보낸 영문 서한의 국문 초고(37쪽) 뒷면에 적혀 있는 글이다.

4 February 1947

The Chairman
Korean Interim Legislative Assembly
Capitol Building
Seoul

Dear Mr. Chairman:

By appointment order signed this day, I have named Mr Ahn Chai Hong as Korean Civil Administrator of the Government of Korea, subject to confirmation of the Legislative Assembly as provided in Ordinance 118. A copy of the order is enclosed herewith.

Because of the importance of this appointment in fulfilling our purpose to increase to the maximum the functions and responsibility of Korean officials of the government, it is requested that the Legislative Assembly give this appointment its earliest possible consideration.

Sincerely yours,

ARCHER L. LERCH
Major General United States Army
Military Governor in Korea

Lt. Gen. John R. Hodge

Dear General Hodge,

I wish to express my appreciation of the
confidence you have ~~expressed~~ shown in offering me
~~the~~ nomination to the office of Civil Administrator.
I regard the office as one in which great
contribution can be made to the welfare
and advancement of the people.

The duties of the office are not
clearly set out: I assume that it is
intended that it shall carry adequate
authority to meet its obvious responsibilities.
I am stating herein a few observations that
I regard as of importance, in this connection.

First, it is of vital moment that the
Interim Legislature should be strengthened, and
the hands of those who work with you should
be upheld. The unoccupied seats should be
promptly filled.

※《민세안재홍선집》 제2권에 "하지미군사령관에 보낸 공한 — 민정장관 취임 수락에 앞서"란 이름으로
실려 있다. 선집에는 1947년 3월 2일자로 되어 있으나 민정장관 취임 전인 2월 초로 추정된다.

ned, the various departments should be coordinated under the primary administrative responsibility of the Administrator; it goes without saying that the last authority of decision must remain in the Military Governor and the Commanding General,

A gradual change of personnel, in the interests of better and more efficient government should be contemplated, again subject to the qualifications above stated

The reorganization and decrease of departments, bureaus and offices is necessary, with the objectives of budget reform and elimination of overlapping and duplication, and the centering of responsibility for government operation in clearly recognized sub-heads.

The opinion of the Civil Administrator should be respected with regard to the problems of the people's economic well-being

To meet the difficulties caused by the fact

that Koreans, other than those who collaborated
with the enemy, are not experienced in
administration, there should be established an
Administrative Investigation Committee,
under the direct supervision of the Civil
Administrator.

The problems confronting us will remain
many and difficult, but they are not
insuperable. With mutual confidence and
with continued effort, we shall succeed in
the attainment of all our objectives.

HEADQUARTERS
United States Army Military Government In Korea
Office of the Military Governor
Seoul, Korea

12 March 1947

MEMORANDUM TO: Mr. Ahn Chai Hong

There are rumors going around that you are looking for replace-
ments for certain directors. Those rumors are causing damage to morale.
I wish you to do all in your power to prevent such rumors. There are
so many other important things crying for action. Let us get those
things accomplished first. We must go slowly on personnel changes
and not get everybody stirred up over rumors.

ARCHER L. LERCH
Major General, United States Army
Military Governor

WAR DEPARTMENT
WASHINGTON, D. C.

17 March 1947

Mr. Ahn Chai Hong
Civil Administrator
U. S. Military Government
APO 235, Care Postmaster
San Francisco, California

Dear Mr. Ahn:

May I congratulate you on your new place in the Government of Korea, although I feel that the Military Government is the one really to be congratulated on having secured a man of your stature to fill this most important position.

The Civil Administrator has it in his power to do a tremendous amount of progressive work for the good of Korea. I am convinced that there could not have been found a man whose patriotism, interest and ability surpassed yours. I congratulate you and am confident that your efforts will bring great progress to South Korea.

You have the responsibility of coordinating the efforts of the several departments of this Interim Government of Korea. The departments are staffed by outstanding Koreans, whose enthusiasm has worked wonders in developing their departments. I know these gentlemen very well, consider them my finest Korean friends, and have faith in their ability. It is amazing what progress they have made since September 1945 and it is most gratifying to realize what trained Koreans can do when they are given the opportunity. I am confident that you, in your position as Civil Administrator, can weld together a team which will form the foundation for a successful independent government of Korea. I wish you and them the greatest of success. I know that you will have their full support and will be able to direct them to bigger and better production.

I have just had the opportunity to talk with General Hodge here in Washington concerning conditions in Korea since I departed last fall. I am glad to find that continued progress is being made. At times there is suspicion that more can be done, but when reviewing the progress over the period of a year and a

45

half, I, personally am much pleased with what I observe.

       I am particularly interested in the work being done by
the Legislature. I anticipated that there might be difficulty in welding together a group of Koreans from all over
South Korea. I expected that they would make mistakes, but
in doing so, would learn rapidly their duties in this most
important body representing South Korea. I regret their action on the subject of trusteeship. It is most unfortunate
to let this subject arise in public debate in the Legislature.
It should only be a matter of concern after the Provisional
Government has been established. Such unwise action by the
Legislature can have no helpful effect on the future of Korea
and only harms the reputation of Koreans in the eyes of the
other nations. There is a particular time when the subject
of trusteeship must be considered and that is when it is
definitely known what trusteeship means. There are so many
other extremely important subjects which must be considered by
the Legislature that it is unfortunate to take time on such an
intangible and disturbing topic as trusteeship. Koreans need
a unified country; they need a unified spirit to make themselves ready for their independent government. Every effort
must be made by the Koreans themselves to develop this national
unified spirit - this teamwork, which is so necessary for a
good government. They, the Legislature, must not lose sight
of the goal toward which all of Korea must go. It must show
the world that Koreans can work together for the good of their
country, and on assignments which are vital and constructive.
It is necessary that the Legislature develop the regulations
for national elections and develop an educational program so
that every Korean will understand the responsibilities of citizenship. There must be effort made to stabilize the food situation so that South Korea can become self-sufficient lest
there be suffering for lack of food. There must be a solution
to the problem of over-population, and the settlement of displaced persons coming into the country from overseas. There
are many problems of education and sanitation which require
doing. Every effort must be made with the least possible delay
to develop South Korea for independence. This is the responsibility of the Legislature and I trust that they will not lose
sight of this objective. They must not be discouraged by the
efforts of short-sighted persons who fail to realize the large
responsibilities of the Legislature and who propose action harmful to Korea.

General Hodge has been very fortunate in his visit here
to have some very fine publicity for Korea. He has talked
to many persons in our Government and in our industry. He
has presented a very clear picture of Korea and her needs.
He has been met on every hand with sympathetic understanding.
If the Koreans will continue their fine efforts at rebuilding
their country, if they will cooperate to further the work
which General Hodge has done so well in this country, I am
sure that the results will be outstanding. Unfortunately,
there are Koreans who fail to realize that the United States
is doing its utmost to assist Korea in its efforts toward independence, and with this lack of understanding, are taking
action which is harmful to Korea. I am sorry that this is
happening and trust that it may not continue. There is only
one way to help and that is for all Koreans to give full support to the United States in its effort to solve the Korean
problem. Koreans must not be selfish, must not consider their
individual positions, but must unite in an all-out patriotic
effort for the good of Korea.

I want to apologize for not having written to you sooner.
I regret that I did not see you to say goodbye to you on my
departure from Korea. I want to thank you many, many times
for the beautiful tray, which you were thoughtful enough to
give to Mrs. Arnold. She prizes it highly and is most appre-
ciative of your kindness.

I hope that you will understand my full sympathy for Korea
and her problems. I am always anxious and willing to help in
any way that I can. I trust that that you in your very important
position may be able to develop the highest kind of teamwork in
the Korean Interim Government and that Korea may, under your
guidance, lay a firm economic foundation for its independence.

Please give my best wishes to your staff and to your very
able department heads, whom I remember so pleasantly.

Very sincerely,

A. V. ARNOLD
Major General, USA
Chief Plans Section, AGF

HEADQUARTERS XXIV CORPS
Office of the Commanding General

APO 235
SEOUL, KOREA

27 March 1947

Mr. Ahn Chai Hong
Office of Civil Affairs
Seoul, Korea

Dear Mr. Ahn:

Mrs. Brown and I accept with pleasure your kind invitation to your party at 1730 Monday, March 31st at the Capitol.

Sincerely yours,

ALBERT E. BROWN
Major General, U. S. Army
Commanding

安民政長官 座下

謹啓 今月三十一日下午
立時半에 開催되之
貴下의 宴會에 本官
内外가 參席하고저
하오니 兹以下諒하시옵
소서.

一九四七年三月二七日
朝鮮駐屯美軍司令官 代理
陸軍少將 박라운

MEMORANDUM

At this time of your return for resumption of direct control of policy in Korea, I am taking the opportunity to set out my thoughts on over-all situation and policy governing the immediate future.

I believe that we have made some progress in the two related tasks of educating the people in democratic processes and of building a sound and constructive middle group. A great deal more work remains to be done immediately. On a number of specific points, I shall welcome an opportunity for prompt consultation with you.

I. In the field of Koreanization of the structure of government, it seems likely that the Legislature will pass a measure which can be integrated into our plan, with possible slight alterations. The Legislature will recognize the necessity of continuing governmental supervision of rice collection, and will give full cooperation in the effort to curb inflation and to restore production.

II. Fundamental problems in the laying of democratic foundations still remain to be considered. These are related to the two problems presented by the election law and the law defining pro-Japanese collaborationists.

(a) If we are to succeed in establishing here a sound frame-work of government that will cooperate with American policy and will work effectively for Korean independence, it is necessary that this entire problem be given careful consideration. Some method must be found to cleanse the government of the partisan and frequently corrupt officials who control, at least, all its lower levels. This is fundamental, and it is a part of the task undertaken by the United States and stated in the Moscow Decision, which you have labored to have us accept.

To proceed with immediate general elections for a new governing body before this preliminary work is done would be to misunderstand the fundamental nature of the problem and to substitute the surface aspect of democracy for the reality.

In the present state of affairs, there is no reasonable prospect for free and honest elections in Korea. The work of reform and inculcation must be given precedence before the work of building.

This is not to say that I disapprove of the plan to enact an electoral statute. This should be done promptly, but it should be done upon a plan of staggering elections from the

lowerest to the highest so that the work of reform can begin
where it must begin, on the village level first.

(b) A reform in the Police Department is urgently and
immediately necessary. Under the pretense of breaking the
general strike, the police have arrested wholesale and have
seized the opportunity for vengeance on their personal and
political opponents. Police reform must of necessity be given
the highest priority in our immediate work. It is absolutely
requisite that the police play a neutral part always and every-
where. (See Exhibit 1 attached herewith)

III. The function of the Coalition Committee in government
should be given reconsideration. Our members do not believe
that the Committee should be erected into a super-cabinet. On
the other hand, they do not believe that it should be dissolved.
It should rather be reorganized and broadened into something
sufficiently wide to permit it to serve as a clearing house for
political action, and an organization to which all **really pa-**
triotic and consciencious men can subscribe.

In the interests of widening broader public support, it
is imperative that the aid of the military be given in a plan
designed to grant amnesty to those individuals who are not
criminals but who are the victims, in some cases, of bad judgment
and, in others, of partisan prosecution. By so doing, we can
extend the work of political education, build public confidence,
and take ammunition away from the enemy. (See Exhibit 2)

Furthermore, it is absolutely urgent that the Coalition
Committee should send out special agents or inculcators to promote
and enhance the setting up of Provincial Autonomy Promotion
Associations (or the like) from village up to the provincial
capitals. This is very important in educating and preparing the
people for the elections.

In order to build up a state founded on democratic principles (which we believe is also the policy of America), it is
the mission of the Coalition Committee to strengthen and to en-
large the same, and while enlightening the Rightists on their
fallacy of their concept, and frustrating the partisanship of
the police, we shall also seek to have the extreme Leftists
also liquidate their blind adherence to a foreign dictatorship.
This is our mission and not only we believe it to be possible,
but we also think that it is the only course to follow. To
realize a true democratic state it is necessary to popularize
the meaning of democracy, and to this end a certain trying
interval is inevitable before we can have a genuine democratic
election. To attain this, we want to organize immediately under
the impulse of the Coalition Committee (Provincial Autonomy
Promotion Associations). These Associations or leagues shall

bring to the masses the concept of democracy as democracy is understood by us. The Coalition Committee is trying to fulfill this mission, but the police under the influence of the Rightists are making it well-nigh impossible, and unless the police force is radically reformed there is fear and even certainty that any future elections shall not reflect the sentiment of the people, and that many able leaders shall be barred.

Conclusion

To conclude I shall propose two absolutely necessary conditions, the non-fulfillment of which can only bring dire consequences to South Korea, and with it the utter failure of the M. G.

(1) There must be a reshuffle of the police personnel at least a few of the most notorious ones should be replaced. To the unsuspecting, the police may by attending to their duty of preserving peace and order, but the reality is quite the contrary. Where the police favors one side to the detriment of the other, and where it interferes in political matters, it is impossible to realize democratic ideals. We can give any number of instances where the police have shut their eyes to terrorism and have connived with, if not instigated, terrorist groups. Such state of affairs not only creates a feeling of unrest and mistrust of the M. G., but the plans of the Coalition Committee cannot be realized. Therefore, as already recommended by the Korean--American Joint Conference, the police personnel must be changed--at least some of the district and provincial chiefs.

(2) To postpone the general election to a more proper time. At present time Korea's economy is controlled by the Pro-Japs, and unless the law concerning the Pro-Japs is enacted and acted upon, no patriotic Korean can hope to serve his country. As stated above, only after the police force is reformed can we have a fair election.

CC: Gen. Brown
    Gen. Lerch
    Gen. Helmick
    Gen. Weckerling
    Lt. Bertsch
    Mr. Ahn Jai-Hong

REPORT ON THE ACTUAL CONDITIONS OF THE
NORTH CHOLLA PROVINCE

Public Opinion:

It has been widely propagandized that America has fundamentally changed her foreign policy, that a separate government will be established in South Korea within a month thanks to Dr. Rhee's successful diplomacy, and that this government will participate in the United Nations so as to be able to control even North Korea in future. At the same time, the Coalition Committee has been propagandized by the right wing parties as a reactionary, treacherous group.

A. Iri District

The newly appointed Mayor of Iri, Kim Byoung-soo, who is the adviser of the Han Kook Democratic Party and Secretary General of the Iksan County Branch of Dr. Rhee's O. H. Q., emphasized in his speech at the mass meeting for the March First Celebration, that people should not be cheated by Kimm Kiu-sic and his men who claimed that the anti-trusteeship movement should be staged after establishing the provisional government, and that no lecture should be allowed to the youth in this district by Kang who is Kimm's follower. It is said even the police are under the new mayor's control. The following is an actual case of violence committed by the police:

A christian called Bak, who is an officer of the Y. M. C. A. [Young People's Christian] Federation of Iksan County and church member, took off a poster from the wall in a dark night and read what was written on it. There he found "Absolute Anti-Trusteeship". As soon as he took the poster off, a score of young men began to strike him. He was surrounded by them and was beaten nearly to death. When he was taken to the police station by them, the police in charge, who had been a detective under the Japanese regime, detained this heavily wounded man at the police station and let the others go. Upon hearing this news, not only the pastor and elders of of the church, but also Mr. Yang Yoon-mook, Chairman of the Branch of the Korean Independence Party, testified that the man in question was a vigorous, patriotic right wing youth standing firmly against the trusteeship. However, the police did not care about their testimony. When the Y. M. C. A. [Federation] men visited the Secretary General of the Han Kook Democratic Party and told him of the incident, the latter said: "As the Federation belongs to Dr. Kimm and the young man detained by the police is greatly influenced by Kang who is Dr. Kimm's follower, I think it is necessary to investigate thoroughly the arrested man." Thus, Bak who is in a critical condition is still detained at the police station.

B. Keumjei District

In spite of the strict surveillance of the police during curfew hours, terrorists have raided leftists' houses at midnight. People could not but wonder how these terroristic activities could have occurred during curfew hours. As a result, a feeling of unrest is prevailing among the inhabitants.

C. Booan and Kot'chang Districts

According to reliable sources, the right wing youth groups in cooperation with the police destroyed many houses belonging to leftists. Whenever the rich did not contribute enough money, as much as they were asked, their houses were destroyed too. Consequently, both the rich and the poor, right and left, are terror-stricken.

PEOPLE'S GENERAL POLITICAL TENDENCY

I had contact with many patriotic young men from Chunchoo and Chungeup. It seems that the populace have been freed from the pressure of the Communists, but they are now under the pressure of the right wing parties. The present condition is causing them believe that the political course defined by Dr. Kimm and Mr. Lyuh is the only road to follow by the Koreans. If no more violence is committed by the police, all the patriotic forces will eventually merge into a united front.

Even though the reformation of the police cannot be realized at present, the populace are ready to organize a united front by April 20 as they can bear no longer the present conditions, and they hope Dr. Kimm will come out to accord them due assistance in this connection.

Reported by:

Kang Won-yong

To: Dr. Kiusic Kimm
The Chairman of the Interim Legislative Assembly
of South Korea

Dear Dr. Kimm:

We submit to you for your information the following
report obtained from a general survey of the public opinion
in the city of Seoul.

REPORT

QUESTION: WHAT METHOD DO YOU DEEM TO BE DEMOCRATIC IN
PRACTICING THE LAND REFORM POLICY IN SOUTH KOREA?

ANSWER: (Transcription from the original shorthand record)

1. By "democratic practice" is meant the abolition of the
feudalistic system of control of farm, the confiscation
of these properties free to farmers, who constitute the
the majority of the Korean people.

National stabilization and rehabilitation may be expected
when the farming class, as contrasted with the minority who are
land owners, become more prosperous.

The enemy lands which are owned by traitors and pro-
Japanese are of course to be confiscated without any compensation and given to farmers free; and the rest owned by Koreans who
should be bought by the Government at the minimum price, thus
insuring and improving their livelihood.

In case this policy is put into realization, the Government may meet some financial difficulties. The Government
can, however, overcome them by adapting some proper tax system.
If put in force, this land reform policy will eventually benefit
the political coalition movement, which is, at present time,
making slow progress. This policy will also have a vital and
idealistic meaning in the establishment of a unified Government. (80 o/o)

2. Confiscation of the farm lands without compensation,
and free distribution. (20 o/o)

CONFIDENTIAL

南 朝 鮮 過 渡 政 府

（ 美 軍 地 域 ）

SOUTH KOREA INTERIM GOVERNMENT

（USA ZONE）

10 May 1947

MEMORANDUM FOR: Mr. Ahn, Chai Hong, Civil Administrator.

There are inclosed papers which were forwarded to me by the

Commanding General, XXIV Corps, asking for my recommendations.in

certain alleged activities of Dr. Kimm, Kiusic.

I desire that you cause further confidential personal investiga-

tion to be made of the matter either through Police channels, Depart-

ment of Justice channels or such other channels as you may elect.

Certainly the investigation should include an opportunity by Dr. Kimm,

Kiusic to make such statement as he desires. Following your investi-

gation, I desire to have your confidential report including your con-

clusions and recommendations.

ARCHER L. LERCH
Major General, United States Army
Military Governor

Incls.

── 統一한 自主獨立朝鮮을 爲하야 ──

FOR A FREE, UNITED, INDEPENDENT KOREA

CONFIDENTIAL

In the forenoon of 8 April 1947, Chief Police Chang of the
Metropolitan Police and Captain Lee of the Bon Chung Police Station
came to this office and made a verbal report to the following effect:

Lee Pomsung (41 years old), Kim Pyung Kiun (40 years old) and
Lee Sajik (41 years old) collected money from Lee In Jik and ten
other persons with the promise that they could secure Japanese
refugees' baggages so that they could make an enormous amount of
profit. The total sum involved is 19,110,000 yen. With this money
Lee donated, according to his confession, 4,200,000 yen in hard cash
to Dr. Kimm and put up a deposit of 8,000,000 in the Bank of Chosen
with the names of Dr. and Madam Kimm. Moreover, he confessed that
he paid out Dr. Kimm's debt which he owed to the Chosen Savings Bank.
He also gave a sum of 330,000 yen to Mr. Koo Sung, a go-between
between Dr. Kimm and Lee himself. The three promoters are now
detained in Bon Chung Police Station and are being investigated by
the police authorities.

In the early part of the morning Chief Prosecutor, Lee In,
telephoned to the Police Captain asking the Captain to drop the
case entirely because Dr. Kimm is going to refund the money at
noon 8 April.

About 1230 9 April the go-between, Koo, came into this office
and confessed that there was a deposit of 8,000,000 yen in the Cho
Heung Bank; 6,000,000 under the name of Madam Kimm and 2,000,000
under the name of Dr. Kimm. Madam Kimm wanted to use 3,000,000 for
Presbyterian Girls' School and the other 3,000,000 for the Orphanage.
The money was deposited on 17 February and it was returned on 7 March,
after having found out that the promoter, Lee, had used Dr. Kimm's
name right and left in collecting large sums of money from various
persons.

Although 8,000,000 was returned to Lee, there is still a gap
of 3,000,000 yen which Dr. Kimm and Mr. Won spent for the cause of
the Coalition Committee. The go-between says that if the promoter,
Lee, is released from the Police Station, then he can make some
arrangement so that those that have given money to him should be
paid back. He, furthermore, hopes that the case should be investigated in secret so that the prominent leader's name should not be
dragged in it. As the thing stands, if the police conduct that
investigation very carefully, there may not be any chance of making
this case known to the public, but the danger lies in the fact that
those who are deceived by the promoter come to Dr. Kimm's headquarters
and ask him to refund the money.

56

HEADQUARTERS
OFFICE OF THE ASSISTANT DIRECTOR &
CHIEF OF THE METROPOLITAN POLICE
SEOUL, KOREA

9th April 1947.

SUBJECT : Fraud Case in the name of Big Person.

TO   : Colonel Maglin
            Dr. Chough

            Directors,
            Department of Police

            Suspects : Lee Bum Sung, 41 yrs of age of 26 Kang Gi Jung,
                       Young San.
                       Occupation - President, Chosun Wage Enterprise Co.

                       Kim Byung Gyun, 40 yrs of age of 98 He Wa Dong.
                       Occupation - Manager, Chosun Enterprise Co.

                       Lee Sa Jik, 41 yrs of age of 399-4 Shin Dang Dong.
                       Occupation - Manager, Chosun Enterprise Co.

        FACTS : In the middle of September 1946, the above Three
suspects organized the Chosun Enterprise Co. (a bogus, fictitions Co.)
with no funds whatsoever. They took advantage of the present economic
confusion and shortage of commodities, conspirated together to earn
thousands of yen in one scoop, dreaming of becoming instant millionaires.

        They therefore spread various false propagandas stating
that their Company would purchase salt, copper and Japanese bundles from
Military Government at cheap prices by using the name of Dr. Kim Kiu
Shic. Commencing last October till Febuary of this year, they defrauded
Mr. Lee In Jik and 10 other persons by written contracts of 19,110,000
yen promising to purchase, resell and deliver the required amount of
commodities in due time.

        Attached sheet shows the specification of how the
fraudulent money was used.

STRICTLY CONFIDENTIAL

SPECIFICATION OF FRAUDULENT MONEY SPENT

```
 1.  Purchased - Korean house - 160 Ok Chun Jung         225,000 yen
 2.       "          Ship                               1,082,800
 3.       "          600 sets of quilts                 1,800,000
 4.       "          Furnitures for Living Room             70,000
 5.  Paid - in to Dr. Kim Kiu Shik.                     4,200,000
 6.    "    "   "  "       "    "    "  for purchase of Auto.   70,000
 7.  Contributed to M. G. Labour Department                30,000
 8.       "       " Han Mi (America-Korea) Association    200,000
 9.       "       " Hung Jin's Political Party            100,000
10.       "       " Chosun Canned Goods Association        30,000
11.  Loaned to Park Sun Cheol, Mgr. of Minakai Cloth Fact. 150,000
12.    "      " Seoul Construction Firm                   100,000
13.  Contributed to "Min Chung" (Communist) Party         30,000
14.  Deposited in Dr. Kim Kyu Shik's account at Chosun Bank 8,000,000
15.  Loaned to Mr. Kim Jin Ho, living at Chong No, 1st Bl. 135,000
16.  Presented to Mr. Min Woon Shik, Chief of Information,
     Labour Dept. M.G. and Mr. Chang Hong Yeon, Instruction
     officer, same department.                            70,000
17.  Payroll of employees of Chosun Enterprise Co.       175,000
18.  Reception and Business expenses                     670,000
19.  Contributed to Coalition Committee                  200,000
20.  Paid - in to Dr. Kim Kiu Shik for payments of his
                 debts at the Chosun Saving Bank         130,000
21.  Paid to Mr. Son Jung Ho                             500,000
22.  Paid - in to Mr. Ku Sung, Dr. Kim's man             330,000
23.  Paid to Mr. Chung Nam Ik                            480,000
24.  Invested in the Tooth Powder Co.                    130,000
25.  Lee Bum Sung's Personal Expenses                    102,200


                          TOTAL   :      19,010,000 yen
```

SPECIFICATION OF FRAUDULENT MONEY PAID IN TO DR. KIM KIU SHIK.

1. On November 7th 1946, Suspect Lee Sung Bum paid 50,000 yen to
    Mrs. Kim Kiu Shik at her residence.

2. In the middle of November 1946, Suspect Lee paid 200,000 yen
    of Chosun Industrial Bank cheques to Dr. Kim Kiu Shik.

3. In November again, Suspect Lee paid 70,000 yen through Mr. Ku
    Sung, one of Dr. Kim's man to Mrs. Kim Kiu Shic.

4. Towards the end of November 1946, Suspect Lee paid 130,000 yen
    in cheques to Dr. Kim Kiu Shik.

5. On Three different occasions, between November and December 1946,
    Suspect Lee paid to Mrs. Kim Kiu Shik a total of 100,000 yen.

6. In the beginning of December 1946, Suspect Lee paid in to Dr. Kim
    Kiu Shik, 400,000 yen.

7. In the end of December 1946, Mr. Ku Sung and Suspect Lee deposited
    2,000,000 yen in the Cho Heung Bank in Dr. Kim's account.

8. In the beginning of January 1947, Mr. Ku Sung and Suspect Lee
    deposited 1,000,000 yen in the Cho Heung Bank in Dr. Kim's account.

9. On Febuary 17th 1947, Mr. Ku Sung deposited 8,000,000 yen in the
    Cho Heung Bank in Dr. Kim's account.

10. Towards the end of Febuary 1947, on 5 or 6 occasions, Suspect Lee
    through Mr. Ku Sung paid in to Dr. Kim a total of 300,000 yen.

    Total of Fraudulent Money received by Dr. Kim Kiu Shik - 12,250,000 .

LIST OF VICTIMS AND AMOUNT OF DEFRAUDED MONEY.

Date	Victim	Sum	
Early Oct. 1946	Chang Sung Kun	100,000 yen	
Middle " "	Shul Yun Woo	150,000	
" " "	Yun Ki Dong	300,000	
Early November 1946	Kim Byung Kei	300,000	
" " "	Lee Jong Tai	500,000	Recovered 200,000
Middle " "	Kim Ung Chul	300,000	
End of " "	Kim Mok Ung	500,000	
	Jung Nam Ik	2,500,000	
	Kim Jae Ha	3,660,000	
	Son Chung Ho	2,000,000	
Febuary 17th 1947	Son Jung Ho	2,800,000	

TOTAL : 19,110,000 yen.

T. S. CHANG
Assistant Director
Chief of the Metropolitan Police.

145-6 Sam Chung Tong
Seoul, Korea
7 May 1947

Maj. Gen. Archer L. Lerch, U.S. Army
Military Governor, USAMGIK
Capitol Building
Seoul, Korea

Dear Gen. Lerch;

    Your good letter of 6 May 1947 with a copy attached of a report by Gen. Weckerling concerning a statement by myself on the case of Lee Pum-Sung was received with appreciation.

    I would make a few comments however concerning points mentioned in your letter as well as in the report as of my statement.

    First, No conference was held actually between Gen. Weckerling and myself on 22 April 1947 on this or any other matter. The fact was that I had a chat with Lt. Bertsch and gave him the gist of such a statement on the date mentioned, though I made no record of the exact date and I gave only a verbal account. I therefore have made a few corrections or additional comments on the so-called statement by me, which will speak for themselves.

    You state that Gen. Hodge has asked you ... ... to request that I make every effort possible to see that the repayment is made. Am I to understand that I personally should make the repayment or make effort towards Lee and Koo, if they are the real offenders of the law , to repay? If the first is intimated, I think I am first of all entitled to know who precisely are my debtors and to what amounts, even though I had the ability to pay. Furthermore, I should be entitled to have proper vouchers and orders making me responsible for the payment or "repayment". As to the actual amount received by me, it was ¥4,000,000, as the bank books will show. Although I have had reports that the total amounts involved was ¥16,000,000 and some claimants say it was ¥18,000,000, I am still at sea as to what was the total amount involved. If Gen. Hodge means that I should try to make Lee, or Lee and Koo together, repay, I do not see how I shall be able to do this when I have no access to these persons------Lee, I understand, is arrested and I do not even know whether Koo is still at large or not. Concerning the sums I have drawn and spent from the above mentioned ¥4,000,000, I can show my bank books and vouchers that not a cent has been used for personal purposes. In other words, every cent was spent in what may be called my political activities, mainly, in conjuntion with the operations of the Coalition Committee and the Interim Legislature, such as payments for entertainments and other general operational expenses

    I should be grateful to know Gen. Hodge's and your further pleasure on this matter.

                         Yours very sincerely,

                              Kiusic Kimm

P.S: I have obtained by telephone permission from Gen. Weckerling
to make the corrections and comments on the copy of the report
mentioned, which I return herewith to you.

     Enclosure: Copy of Gen. Weckerling's Report.

CC: Gen. Hodge
    Gen. Brown
    Gen. Weckerling
    Mr. Ahn Chai-Hong
    Lt. Bertsch

南 朝 鮮 過 渡 政 府

（美 軍 地 域）

SOUTH KOREA INTERIM GOVERNMENT

（USA ZONE）

12 May 1947

安 在 鴻 民 政 長官 貴下

MEMORANDUM FOR: Mr. Ahn Chai Hong, Civil Administrator.

李 範 燮 事件에 關하여는 아래

1. With reference to the case of Lee, Bum Sung, I desire that

事件에 言及하는 바와 如히, 合法 않은 此 事件에

you tell the Police and the Department of Justice to proceed to in-

關係된 者는 全部 調査하여 即時 處斷하도록

vestigate and prosecute at once all persons involved in illegal acts

警務部 와 司法部에 命令하여 주실 것.

except as otherwise herein indicated.

此 件에 關 係된 軍政官吏에 對하여는 貴官

2. I desire that you personally cause a thorough investigation

이 直接 嚴密한 調査 하되 어데 까지나 公正

to be made of all charges made against Government officials. This in-

한 것이고 그들의 地位 如何를 不拘하고 特

vestigation should be thorough and impartial, but it must be understood

典을 줄수는 없을 것 임니다.

that no Government official has any immunity because of his Government

status.

此 件에 있어서 받은 돈은 全部 本 所有者

3. It is desired that steps be taken to return all money now

에게 返 還하도록 할 것 임니다.

held by anyone to individuals to whom it properly belongs.

ARCHER L. LERCH
Major General, United States Army
Military Governor

── 統 一 한 自 主 獨 立 朝鮮 을 爲하 야 ──

FOR A FREE, UNITED, INDEPENDENT KOREA

13 May 1947

民政長官 安在鴻 閣下

MEMORANDUM FOR: Mr. Ahn Chai Hong, Civil Administrator.

하지 將軍이 方수 電話로 本官에게 말하기를

General Hodge just called me and suggested that you ask Mr.

貴下께서 崔東昨氏나 尹琦燮氏에게 말슴하여

Chai Dong Oh or Mr. Yun Ki Sup to appoint a Committee of Legislators

李範声事件에 關聯되여 있는 立法議員에 对한

to investigate charges made against members of the Assembly in connec-

院内 調查委員会를 任命하시기를 提議하여 왓슴니다

tion with the Lee Pum Sung case. 토록

ARCHER L. LERCH
Major General, United States Army
Military Governor

軍政長官
陸軍少將   아ー취 · 엘 · 라ー취

Use Dept of Justice if
you wish

A L L
5/13/47

Mr. Ahn Chai Hong:

You have authority to investigate the entire Lee Pum Sung case, and all involved by using any agency under your jurisdiction.

G. L. L
5/13/47

「假名は平假名で明瞭に」

朝鮮金融組合聯合會原稿用紙

C, I, C, 에서 記述한 覺書(大同으로 强要함으로 正記述함)

一, 閔○은 安在鴻、柳東悅과「푸라이스」大佐와「깟소」少佐를 親衛部에서 고만두게 하라고 計劃함이다.

二,「푸라이스」大佐가 조치못했고「푸라이스」大佐보다 더 高級인 士官에게 말하지 안햇다.

三, 此事件으로「푸라이스」大佐가「푸라이스」大佐보다 더 高報인 士官과 不和하게 된 것에 對하야는 責任이 우리에게 있다.

四、親衛部再組織計劃은 安在鴻의 金部 軍政長官「러ー취」將軍에게 말하지 안코 狀治하얏다.

五.「푸리이스」大佐와「깟소」少佐를 親衛部에서 고만두게함은「러ー취」軍政長官에 말하라 하얏고 親衛部再組織計劃中 一部分은 重要한 秘密로 官에 말하라하얏고 親衛部再組織計劃中 一部分은 重要한 秘密로

〔軍式組〕

20字×10行＝200字詰

하기로하얏다

六、航衛部再組織、秘密計劃과責任者는 一、安在鴻 二、柳東悅 三、

關西黨이다

一九四七年五月十五日

　　　　右關西黨

「假名は平假名で明瞭に」

朝鮮金融組合聯合會原稿用紙

（筆式紙）

20字×10行＝200字詰

「假名は平假名で明瞭に」

朝鮮金融組合聯合會原稿用紙

・乙、工、己의 覺書說明

(一)는 中止訊問은 問題된것・이는
것이 强制로 問題이된다.

(二)은 道德上問題로오히려 이러케된
것은 自己이고는것이다.

(三)은 道德上 繼續問題

(四)는 問題없다.

(五)가 一方問題야. 一部分秘密로는 何故로 記載안했나는의 解釋에 何意義을으로

이것은 기타 課長官에게 秘密로記載안는것을 黃意味로 解釋도되고

軍事上問題이 秘露이니것고도 外部에 解釋이된다

味로 述한없은 尚書에 對意味로도 解釋이된다. 一生은 後者의 意味

高尚意味로도되는주있다 그러나 述書로

뭐그러나 檢軍에게 秘露로記한도되니 問題안이된다.

內을 囚)此는 軍政되야 秘密計劃은 軍事上關係로 秘密이니 못解釋이되고 民政長官 軌道新이長 連絡되야 三人이 責任것으로 安心하야 別로問題없다.

朝鮮金融組合聯合會原稿用紙

US - USSR Joint Commission,
Seoul, Korea.

2 June 1947

Mr. AHN, Chai Hong,
Civil Administrator,
The Capitol,
Seoul, Korea.

Dear Mr. AHN:

Mrs. Weckerling and I greatly regretted that we were unable to attend your cocktail party on May 31.

The meeting of the Joint Commission did not adjourn until a late hour on Saturday, and I am sure that you will understand. Otherwise, we would have been delighted to be present.

We wish to extend our thanks to you for your thoughtfulness in remembering us.

Most sincerely,

JOHN WECKERLING,
Brig. General, U.S.A.

南 朝 鮮 過 渡 政 府

（ 美 軍 地 域 ）

SOUTH KOREA INTERIM GOVERNMENT

(USA ZONE)

8 July 1947

Mr. Ahn, Jai Hong
Civil Administrator
South Korea Interim Government
Seoul, Korea.

My dear Mr.Ahn:

Thank you for the very beautiful gift of flowers which you

presented to me on July 4th, our American Independence Day.

Your gift caused me to realize the blessing of an inde-

pendent democratic country, achieved through labor and sacrifice.

I look forward to the same blessing for your country, and am

sorry that it has not yet been achieved. However, it is a pleasure

to work with you toward that goal.

May the day soon come when we will celebrate a free,

united, democratic Korea!

Sincerely yours,

C. G. HELMICK
Brigadier General, United States Army
Acting Military Governor

── 統一한 自主獨立朝鮮을 爲하야 ──

FOR A FREE, UNITED, INDEPENDENT KOREA

WAR DEPARTMENT
WAR DEPARTMENT SPECIAL STAFF
CIVIL AFFAIRS DIVISION
WASHINGTON 25, D. C.

14 July 1947

Mr. Ahn Chai Hong
Seoul Administrator
South Korean Interim Government
Seoul, Korea

Dear Mr. Ahn:

I have been intending to write to you for some time, but have been quite busy. While we are not going to get all we have asked for, I believe that there will be sufficient money contained in the regular Army Appropriation Act to carry us over, at least until the next meeting of Congress.

One of the most difficult fights I have had here was to make final clearance for the Export Import Program. I believe everything is in hand and tomorrow is the opening date. In my opinion, the opening of the Export Import Program should mean a lot to Korea.

It appears to me that one of the biggest things we should do in the near future is to make every effort to improve our fisheries. Fisheries provide unlimited assets. There is a limit to the amount of food which we can raise on the soil; there is no limit to the amount of food we can take from the ocean. I have tried to emphasize our need for fishing craft, fishing nets, and other such equipment.

Please give my kindest regards to all members of the Cabinet. I shall make an effort to write to them individually.

With kindest regards, I am

Sincerely yours,

ARCHER L. LERCH
Major General, USA

24 July 1947

<u>Some jottings for Inspectionary Party of American Press Men</u>

I should like to show my respect to you American press men leading
the opinion of America, and to dedicate the following jottings for your
political information of high grade.

1. It is requested to establish a provisional government uniting North
and South Korea through the success of the US-USSR Joint-Commission.
It is anticipated that Russia will initiate a conciliation of US and
USSR in solving the issue of Korea as far as America and Russia can
not immediately commence hostilities. It is, furtheremore, the principle
on the part of Russia to lay stress on European issues while regarding
the Korean question as secondary. Therefore, the US-USSR Joint-Commission
is very likely to be successful.

The cooperation between US and USSR through the US-USSR Joint-
Commission only will form a consolidated base of the assisstance for the
independence of Korea and the future friendship between Korea and America.

An action on the part of America to establish the so-called South
Korea Seperated Government could be taken in the worst case. It is feared,
however, that there would be a possibility to providr Korea and America with
an unfavourable chance which is apt to alinate one from the other on the
way to establish the seperated government.

2. Early in September, 1945, when the American occupational Forces
marched into Korea, there was established the People's Republic which had the
pro-Russian leanings and was controlled by several communists.

America, on the other hand, kept a too closer collaboration with
Rightists to prevent this leaning of leftists from being vigorous. Even
now there is a little influence of the leftwing, but administration, justice
and police have in the grasp of the extreme right wing.

Unless the patriotic neutral camp(patriotic moderatists) will be hereafter supported, it is feared that people at large would rather be for the left
wing by taking advantage of the regime on the part of the extreme rightwing.

Korea earnestly requests for the economic aid from America as well as
the establishment of a united government.

The purchasing power of the Korean people will be augmented and the international friendship between Korea and America will be consolidated through
America's assisstance and cultivation of the Korean economy. Thus these American goods which are not produced in Korea or which are not manufactured at
chief costs in Korea will be purchased by the Koreans more and more. It should
strictly be prohibited, therefore, to give the Koreans an impression that America
makes Korea mere America's market for selling their merchandise without
assisstanting Korean Manufacturing economy.

It is requested that leaders of the various circles in America pay deep
consideration to the things mentioned above.

AHN CHAI HONG
Civil Administrator
South Korea Interim Government

4 Aug. '47

General Charles G. Helmick
Acting Military Governor
South Korean Interim Government

Dear General Helmick:-

In considering the particular political situation in Cholla-Namdo, it is desirable to transfer Mr. Lee, Chang Whan , Chief of the Korean Civil Service Office of the same province ,to a suitable position within the province. Consquently I wish to recommed Mr. Shin,Chul Kyun as the chief of the Office of KCS of the same province in order to give Mr. Park, Keun Won, the new governor, an opportunity to carry out his duties efficiently.

Respectfully Yours,

Approved :

General Charles G .Helmick   AHN CHAI HONG
Acting Military Governor   Civil Administrator
South Korean Int. Governt.

Dr. Edgar A J. Johnson
Chief Adviser

26 August 1947

Dear Dr. Ahn,

Thank you for the beautiful lacquer box. It is very lovely and I know I will enjoy using it in my new house when I am settled.

Thank you again for remembering me with such a wonderful gift.

Sincerely,
Jacqueline Schaper

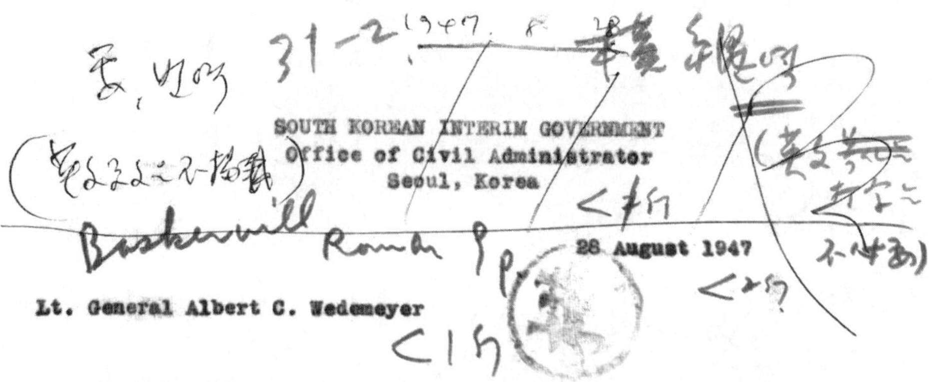

SOUTH KOREAN INTERIM GOVERNMENT
Office of Civil Administrator
Seoul, Korea

28 August 1947

Lt. General Albert C. Wedemeyer

Dear Gen. Wedemeyer,

1. No too much importance can be attached to Korea which is of great moment politically and strategically in the Orient from the viewpoint of the Pacific policy on the part of the United States of America.

2. Russia's invasive ambition which was originated under the reign of the Russian Empire has caused us to have the utmost fear against Russia. Since Russia is a strong, adjacent country to Korea, we think that the best policy to insure Korea's independence is to be jointly guaranteed by America, Russia, England, and China in accordance with the cooperation on the part of the said four countries. ⟨In case the four countries⟩ cooperation should not absolutely be expected, we demand the seperate action as the secondary way in South Korea.

3. It is requested that the following several points be specially be taken notice of in aiding Korea.

    a. In September in 1947 when the American Occupational Forces marched into Korea, there had already been established the Korean People's Republic(CHOSUN IMMIN KONG HWA KOOK) by a small number of communists, and artifice of them was great.
    In order to adjust the then situation, the US Forces intended to cooperate with the influence of the right wing while they proclaimed Military Administration.

    The conservative extreme right wing people have since been closely conciliated with US Military Government, and they have been doing their best to secure the interests of their own classes or parties. They have grasped all the powers of administration, police, and justice (though it is admitted that some left wing men are not-openly sandwiched between the right wing persons), thus virtully holding sway over Military Government. On the other hand, the communistic elements also have been incessantly intrigued against US Military Government.

    Therefore, Military Government officials of the right wing, both in Central and provincial, have frequently used too strong hands over communists while submitting too much exaggerated reports regarding the danger and scales of plots caused by communistic people.
    Consequently it seems that US Military Government are supporting the influence of the extreme right wing while bringing pressure to bear upon the people at large. This tendency has caused much to aliente the populace from US Military Government.

    A very few persons of the neutral political leanings are now holding greatly positions in the goverment, but they have been unable to fully display their political ability under restraints and slanders of a great many extreme right wing persons. The political situation, thus, is growing worse to worse.

    Therefore, the present situation of Korea should be justly grasped

---

※ 이 자료는 《민세안재홍선집》 제2권에 "웨드마이어"란 이름으로 실려 있으나 1947년 8월 2일자로 잘못 기록되어 있다.

while she being economically aided. As far as patriotic persons of
the neutral political leanings, on the other hand, should not be
permitted to control the politics of Korea, continuance of the pressure upon the masses on the part of the extreme right wing will
automatically make the populace turn to and support the left wing,
and the future of Korea would thus be so much disturbed to become
uncontrollableas well as America's policy toward would face a great
danger.

     The Koreans do not like communism. The rampancy, however, of the
influence of the extreme right wing which is always availing itself of
US Military Government is the only motive by which large number of
people are obliged to follow the left wing.

     b.   The genuine general will of the Koreans is caying for
independence which is jointly guaranteed by America, and Russia through
their cooperation. Unfortunately, if cooperation between America and
Russia should not be realized, and if the extreme right wing should
come to power, it would cause a great danger. It is demanded to pay
much consideration to the fact that the populace should be induced to
and be assembled around the neutral political leanings, and this only
is the best policy to be adopted in order to fundumentally deviate
the masses from the temptation caused by the left wing.

     Next, economically, increased production of food, adjustment of
forests and rivers, re-construction of light indusry by which daily
necessaries of the people are produced, enforcement of electricfaed
facilities, exploitation of fuel such as coal, and of scheelite,
graphite, magnecite, etc., improvement of land and marine means of
transportation, proper push of international trade, and assisstance
to and forstering of the other necessary economic establishment(more
detailed statement of these items will be found in other documents)
-----thus aiming at stabilization of the people's living conditions
and enforcing the defence against North as well as peace maintenance
-----these are the indis pensable items for assisting Korea's independence.

     Since the Koreans are not only fond of peace but also are intel-
ligent and talanted, it is not difficult for the Koreans to insure an
independent country enjoying her self-government through economic aid.

     The problem of Korea is far easier to be solved than that of
China if cooperation between America and Russia could be realized and
the 38th parallel be abolished.

     Without the complete independence of Korea, not only can not
China enjoy her independence but also there can not be peace in the
Orient.

     As the socially great influence of certain classes in Korea is
very feeble, so it is comparatively easy to re-organize a democratic
economy according to the policy of America here.
     It is of course necessary to democracize Korea, but it is unna-
tural to import into Korea the democracy of America as it is there.

     c.   It is well-known fact that to predict the future of Korea
under the existence of the 38th parallel is not just and appropriate.
To considerablly forster the industry for producing daily necessaries
in Korea which has close connection with China, the states of India,
and South Pacific Islands means the economical independence of Korea.
The economical independence of is to secure the political one of
Korea , and to complete Korea's mission in order to secure international peace through Korea holding responsibility for a part of America's
policy toward Far East.

To bring up such an economic strenth as mentioned above is no other
thing than to strengthen purchasing power of the Koreans through which
the people will be able to import American goods of high grade.

For about 70 years since the amity treaty was concluded between
Korea and America in 1882, we have been enjoying friendship. It is
therefore, sure to eternally maintain friendship henceforth, too.

                              AHN, CHAI HONG
                           Civil Administrator

DEPARTMENT OF STATE

WASHINGTON

OFFICE OF GENERAL WEDEMEYER

Seoul, Korea
30 August 1947

Mr. Ahn, Chai Hong
Civil Administrator
Capitol Building
Seoul, Korea

Dear Mr. Ahn:

I have just received your letter of 29 August 1947, and am glad to have had the opportunity to read some of your views on the situation here in Korea in addition to hearing the presentation which you conducted Friday morning in the Throne Room. It is helpful to the Mission to obtain your views and I will give them careful consideration.

As you know our fact finding Mission is here in Korea for only a little over a week. It is helpful to the Mission to obtain the views of as many individuals and representative groups as is possible within the short time alloted for our stay.

Thank you for your good wishes and your expression of confidence in my country.

Faithfully yours,

A. C. WEDEMEYER
Lieutenant General, U. S. Army

Seoul, Korea
September 14, 1947

Dear Mr. Ahn —

Your kind expression of sympathy is sincerely appreciated and your thoughtful words and visit to me have done much to alleviate the sorrow.

Sincerely,
Florence M. Hersch.

THE FOREIGN SERVICE
OF THE
UNITED STATES OF AMERICA

~~AMERICAN CONSULATE GENERAL~~
Office of the US Political Adviser
Headquarters XXIV Corps,   Seoul.
September 18, 1947.

Dear Mr. Ahn:

The Acting Secretary of State has directed
me to convey to you the appreciation of the
President of the United States for the message
of sympathy you and the department heads of the
South Korea Interim Government so thoughtfully
addressed to him on the death of his mother.

Sincerely yours,

Joseph E. Jacobs
United States Political Adviser

The Honorable

Ahn Chai Hong,

Civil Administrator,

South Korea Interim Government,

Seoul.

THE WHITE HOUSE
WASHINGTON

The President and Mrs. Truman

deeply appreciate your condolences

in their great loss

23 Sept. 1947

Subject : Failure of US-USSR Join°t Commission and Counter-Measure
          to meet Current Situation

     Korea which is now on the way to complete an independent country
for the people through establishemnt of a united country, requests urgently
and earnestly the economic aid rendered by the United States of America
which was the leader of the allied countries. Economic aid is a principal
task to be practiced in aiding Korea for her independence. The fundanmant-
al and greatest result therefore, will not be secured unless the bassis of con-
structing a new fatherland should be ad°justed from various angles. This
decidedly testifies that economic aid does not only have to do with these
problems economic or industrial.

     I should like to express my opinion concerning thses points.

     Some people censure me for my collaboration with the US-USSR Joint
Commission, regarding me as a political heretics, but this is not a right
view.

     The international politics which is full of changeability does not admit
of blind consistancy, which adhers to only one. The last objective consists
in how much changeability one has in politics and policies judging from the
firm standpoint for acquiring independance. Will the United States of America
and Uion of Soviet Socialist Republics cooperate with each other? Will the
two countries, after all, fail in keeping in cooperation?

     It is greatly fortunate for Korea that a united provisional government
could be established by dint of an impartial election through North and
South Korea under the supervision of UN, which would be brought by the
sucess of the General Assembly of UN. In case America and Russia could not
reach any agreement for their cooperation, and there would be a seperate
disposition in South Korea only, it is one of the important national
policies that the people facing General Election in South Korea should be
induced to the real democracy and to hhartily collaborate with the South
Korean Interim Government. T

     The system for establishment of a united country must be consolidated
by increase of reliance upon the government on the part of the people and
of impartiality of law through fair and rigid attitude at such aspects con-
tracting with the populace as admnistration, justice, and police administration, and by fostering staple democratic capacity through North and South Korea
through the people's cooperation and unity based on the desire for completion of an independent country. In order to concretely carry out this system
the following terms are required.

     1. Unification and enforcement of administrative function
          It has been planned to adjust the function of the South Korean
Interim Government through appointment of the Korean Civil Administrator.

2

A powerful Governmental structure based on joint responsibility,however,
has not been established yet through non-existance of the system unifying the
governmental commands and existance of personal and eentrifugal leanings on
the part of Directors of Departments and offices of the government. It is therefore, requested that the governemntal structure should be unified around the
Civil Adminitrator from the original purpose handing the administrative
function over the hands of Koreans.

2. The real,genuin democracy should be fostered and the populace should
be induced to gather around this democracy.

Genuin democracy is the self-discrimination against Communism. Even
its fatherland, these years, Communism has been required to be amended fun-
danmentally. Korea does not require Communism to which prolétarian autocracy
and blooding violence are essential jauuging from her tradition and social
objective conditions; Korea is against Communism which denies independence,
freedom and originality of individuals; thus binding up populace under mechanical totalitarianism, Korea absolutely rejects any biassed reliance upon
one foreign country which is inevitably derived from Communism. The eternal
independence and development of the Korean people will be guanteed only by
completion of the people's emancipation, establishment of an independent
country for the people, and international cooperation based on non-reliance
on any foriegn country. Equality and co-prosperity should be aimed at in
systems and facilities of economy, politics, education, etc., thus a country
and societies for the sake of every individual must be established by exclusion of feudalistic and capitalistic monopolization,—these mean gaining
democracy securing the safe fortune of the people fosver.

The capitalistic democracy which had existed in France, England, and
America up to the World War II depends upon the privileged classes con-
sisting of huge finance, industry, capital, or minor big landlords. The democracy, therefore, is fundanmently different in its intrinsic nature from
the new democracy advocated by me which aims at equality and coprosperity.

Thoughts and principles ought to be coped with and overcome by thoughts
and principles, and, in case any body should break bounds, he must be punished and rectified by invocation of governmental authority. In other words
genuin democracy should be established and ptatised by the government; genuin democracy should support and foster the political influences and advocating
and forcing real democratic platforms and policies to cope with the current
situation while the governmental power should be mobilized to wipe out various
influences contrary to the former. Through such measures as mentioned above,
the populace should be deviated from the unjust fassination of the communist
party and communism, thus inducing them to gather around the patriotic political influence based on complete self-independence of the people. From this
point of view, it is strongly requested to democratize the police administration and to establish just punishment strictly protecting the prestige of
law, thus bringing about reliance on the part of the populace.

3. Constructive solution of the people's living problems—reconstruction
of industry and economy, normal push of foreign trade and proper distribution
of daily necessities.

It is requested that an appropriate measures to mobilize the general
power of the country be established for the purpose of carrying out rehabilitation of insudtry and economy ranging from food, feul, clothes, electricity,
transportation, raw-stuffs, materials, tahchnique, money, and finance; it is

further requested that positive push of foreign trades through barter, and
proper distribution, excluding the profiteering intermediate exploitation, of
of the goods imported from foreign counrties ~and produced at home~ be established. In case we have
effectively displaced ~our country~ our capacity to the utmost, and we are
still in a needy condition, we should properly avail ourleves of the economic aid policy of the United States of America. It is very important for the
execution of this objective to aim at stabilizing and developing the feeling
of the people through a patriotic movement.

Various conscious or unconscious activities of the persons harmful to
the movement for independence, actions which are against this country and the
Koreans and any organizations or individuals destroying law and public peace
must be strictly regulated and overcome.

Since the August 15 in 1945, in South Korea, various dissolute and destructive activities have been openly rampant in the names of democracy or freedom.
The violent activities of the rightists which have been originated from the
viewpoint of revenge over the leftists, have caused a great uneasiness. The
mutual slaughter of the people is very harmful to mutual friendship and love
of the people, (2) lessen mental and material capacity of the people, and(3)
will likely be used as an international denunciation blaming the Koreans for
lack of autonomy and capacity for independence. It is, therefore, required
that such organizations or individuals, as, consciously or unconsciously, habit-
ually pratise or aim at those activities corresponding to(1) (2) (3) mentioned
above should be strictly controlled. It is, consequently, required that, through
this measures, men of the intelligence should be made to return to the real
democratic influence for independence by their new self-examination and new
understanding of the current situation, and men of unintelligence or men who
are wandering ~and~ to have not found the way to be followed should be made to know
direction and destination to be followed.

To carry out these objectives, it is required those people patriotic and
deserving reliance of the public general to appear on, and take charge of various
stages.

5. Enforcement of national defence and peace maintinance structure.
At present, in South Korea, the machninery of national defence is very
poor and in a headless condition, and peace maintenance which is now in charge
of police, comes before general national defence while public peace maintenance
is chiefly lead and kept by the Occupation Army. However, various internal and
international circumstance neckessitates the consolidation of the structure
of national defence.

The national defence of the young and weak Korean people lies in (1)
unity and mutual love, (2) preparation for war time through all-work of the whole
nation, and (3) encouragement of scientification of national defnece.

The unity and mutual love mentioned in (1) completely preventing any
international influence from intruding into Korea, and ,therefore, this fact
should be barne by the people.

The all-work of the whole nation mentioned as (2), will, in peace-time,
guarantee the existance, prosperity, and development of the fatherland in

various circles industrial,cultural,etc.,and in emergency will prevent any invasion from the standpoint of all-nation-war, thus preparing ourselves for the participation of friendly foreign country in the hositilities.

However, South Korea is in needy and non-planned condition in the system of training students and young men, of training military officers, and (e) the other equipments.

By the concentration, through various administrations, of capacity for independence based on democracy a great constructive project must be established and pushed for this purpose. In this respect, too, we must display our capacity to the utmost, and, then avail ourselves of the economic aid rendered by the United States of America.

Since the August 15 in 1945 a great gleam of hope has been shone on us, and experiencing historical emergency. Therrfore, it will greatly effect the eternal fortune of the Koreans whether or not we can conquer this emergency.

30 million brothmen! Let us immediately eliminate all the struggles and oppositions among various classes and camps. Let us immediately stop and liquidate any civil strife trying to take up the veins of government, *let us march forward only for*
and unification and independence.

A split will solidify ruin.

AHN CHAI HONG
Civil Administrator

Subject :
Speech Made by Mr. Ahn, Chai Hong to Korean-American Economic Club,
24 Sept. 1947

Korea which is now on the way to becoming an independent country,
requests urgently and earnestly the economic aid rendered by the United
States of America, which is the leader of the allied countries. Economic
aid is needed in aiding Korea toward her independence. The greatest
results will not be secured unless the basis of reconstructing a new
fatherland should be considered from various angles. This decidedly
intestifies that economic aid does not only have to do with those problems of economy or industry.

I should like to express my opinion concerning these points.

1. Some people censure those who collaborate with the US-USSR Joint
Commission, regarding them as political heretics, but this is not a
just view.

International politics are not consistant but full of changeability.
The object is to find how much changeability one has in politics and
policies in attempting to gain independence. Will the United States of
America and the Union of Soviet Socialist Republics cooperate with each
other or will the two countries, after all, fail in their attempt?

It whould be greatly fortunate for Korea if a United Provisional
Government could be established by dint of an impartial election in
North and South Korea under the supervision of UN , which would be
brought about by the success of the General Assembly of UN. In the
event that America and Russia could not reach an agreement for their
cooperation, and there is a separate disposition made for South Korea
only, it is of national importance that the people of South Korea in

1

facing a general election uphold real democracy and heartily cooperate
with the South Korean Interim Government.

The establishment of a united country must be through an increase
of reliance upon the government on the part of the people and impartiality of law through fair and rigid attitude toward such aspects con-
tactir with populace as administration, justice and police administration and by fostering staple democratic ideals through North and
South Korea through the people's cooperation and unity based on the
desire for a completely independent country. In order to concretely
carry out this system, the following terms are required.

1. Unification and enforcment of administrative function.

It was planned funnel the functions of the South Korean Interim
Government through the Korean Civil Administrator. A powerful govern-
mentstructure, based on joint responsibility however, has not yet
been established due to lack of unification tendencies on the part
in government and existance of personal
of the Directors of Departments and officies of the Government. It is
therefore suggested that the government structure be unified around
the functions of the Civil Administrator, following the original purpose of handing the administrative duties over to the hands of Koreans.

2. Genuine democracy should be fostered and the populace should
be induced to gether around this democracy. Genuine democracy is the
discrimination against Communism. Even in its fatherland, Communism
has been required to amend its policies. Korea does not want Communism
with its proletarian autocracy and bloody violence. Korea is against
Communism which denies independence, freedom and originality of individual ;thus bringing the populace under mechanical totalitarianism.
Korea absolutely rejects any biased reliance upon one foreign country
which is inevitable in communism. The final independence and development of the Korean people will be guaranteed only by completion of
2

the people's emancipation, establishment of an independent country for
and of the people, and international cooperation based on non-reliance
on any foreign country. Equality and co-prosperity shoul1 be aimed at in
fields of economy,politics. education, etc., thus a country dedicated to
the individual must be established by exclusion of feudalistic and capitalistic monopolization, these mean genuine democracy securing the safe
fortunes of the people forever.

The capitalistic democracy which existed in France, England and
America up until World War II depended upon the privileged classes controlling finance, industry, capital or land. The new democracy advocated
by ne is fundamentally different in its intrinsic nature and aims at equality and prosperity for all.

Varying political thoughts and principals must be coped with and won
over by democratic thoughts and principals. In the event anyone breaks
bounds, he must be punished by invocation of governmental authority. In
other words. genuine democracy should be established and practiced by the
government; genuine democracy should support and fester the political influences advocating real democratic platforms and policies to cope with
the current situation while the governmental power should be mobilized
to wipe out various influences contrary to the former. Through such measures as mentioned above, the populace should be deflected from the unjust fascination of the communist party's principles, thus inducing them
to gather around the patriotic democratic ideals based on complete self-
independence of the people. From this point of view, it is strongly requested to democratize the police administration and to establish just
punishment strictly protesting the prestige of law.

3. Constructive solution to the people's living problems, reconstruction of industry and economy, foreign trade, and proper distribution
of daily necessities will be needed.

3

It is requested that appropriate measures to mobilize the general
power of the country be established for the purpose of carrying out rehabilitation of industry and economy, ranging from food, fuel, clothes,
electricity, transportation, paper, shoes, raw-stuffs, materials, techinques
and finances to machinery. It is further requested that a positive push of
foreign trades be made through barter, distribution, excluding the profit-
eeting intermediate exploitation. of goods imported from foreign countries
and those produce at home be established. In the event we have effectively
distributed resources and we are still in a needy condition, we should properly avail ourselves of the economic aid policy of the United States of .
America. It is very important that we develop the democratic feelings of
the people if we are to attain our objectives of stabilization.

4. Various conscious and unconscious harmful activities of persons to
the movement for independence, actions which are against this country and
the Koreans and organizations or individuals destroying law and public
peace must be strictly regulated and overcome.

Since 15 August 1945 there have been in South Korea various destructive
activities openly rampant in the names of democracy and freedom. The violent
activities of the rightists which have originated from the viewpoint of revenge over the leftists have caused great uneasiness. The mutual slaughter
carried on by people of either party is

     (1) very harmful to mutual friendship and love of the people

     (2) lessens mental and material earning capacity of the people

     and (3) will likely be used as an international denunciation, blam-
ing the Koreans for lack of autonomy and capacity for independence. It is,
therefore, required that such organizations or individuals as consiously
practice or aim at those activities coresponding to (1) (2) (3) mentioned
above should be strictly controlled. Men of intelligence should return to
the real democratic ideals of independence by their new self-examination and
4

new understanding of the current situation, and those who are wandering
because they have not found the right direction should be lead to the
right direction.

To carry out these objectives men who are patriotic and deserve the
reliance of the general public will be needed.

5. Enforcement of strength of national defence and the maintenance
of peace

At present, the organization of the national defence in South Korea
is very poor and is in needy condition. The public peace maintenance is
chiefly relied upon the strength of the police, and at present the leading force for the public peace is the status of the Occupational Force.
However, vari us internal and international circumstances necessitate
the adjustment of the structure of the national defence.

The national defence of the young and weak Korean people lie in
(1) unity and mutual love, (2) preparation for war time through labor
of the entire nation, and (3) encouragement of rehabilitation of national defence,

The unity and mutual love mentioned in (1) above would prevent
any international influence on Korea and this fact should be borne in
mind by the people.

Only the labor of the entire nation mentioned in (2) above, will
in peace time guarantee the maintenance of the fatherland, prosperity,
development from the various angles of politics, industry, culture, etc.,
In time of emergency. people with military training will prevent invasion,
and ensure cooperation from friendly nations against the agressors.

However, South Korea is in a needy condition in the system of
training students and young men, of training military officers, and in
equipment.

Constructive democratic administrative action must be taken and ?
5

and pushed for this purpose. In this respect, too, we must exert our capacities to the utmost, and then avail ourselves of the economic aid rendered by the U.S. of America.

Since 15 August 1945 a great gleam of hope has shone upon us. It will greatly affect the future fortune of the Korean nation how we conduct ourselves in this emergency.

30 million brothren!. Let us immediately eliminate all struggle and opposition among various classes and camps. Let us immediately stop civil strife trying to take the reins of government and let us march forward, only forward toward unification and independence!

Division will mean ruin!

AHN CHAI HONG
Civil Administrator

SOUTH KOREAN INTERIM GOVERNMENT
Office of Civil Administrator
Seoul, Korea

5 October 1947

TO : Military Delegation,
Congress of the United States of America,
Seoul, Korea

Gentlemen:

I have the honor of praying for the health of you and the President of the United States of America.

In the West, a bill for the realization of the independence of Korea has been kindly proposed by General Marshall, the Secretary of the State Department is going to be discussed at the General Assembly of the United Nations. In the East, on the other hand, the Chief Commissioner of the Russian Delegation of the US-USSR Joint Commission in Seoul has presented to the Commission the proposal regarding the joint withdrawal of the American and Russian Armed Forces in Korea at the beginning of 1948.

At this period, the members of the Military Committee of the Congress of the United States representing the public opions of the United States of America has come to Korea with military experts to inspect South Korea, occupied by the United States Armed Forces. The barrier of the 38th parallel belt which is now pending and various other problems will be discussed with the heads of the American Occupational Forces here. I clearly understand that this fact will attract the attention of the whole world.

We Koreans have been and will be grateful to you Americans who liberated Korea from the Japanese Empire.

Korea, however, has been divided into two parts by America and

- 1 -

Russia, according to the Yalta Pact. Since 15 August 1945, the United
States of America has faithfully rendered various diplomatic efforts to
fulfill the declaration at Cairo by which the independence of Korea was
publicly promised. Nevertheless, America and Russia have not reached
any agreement as yet. Not only do the Koreans deplore the fact, but also
you Americans too, I am sure, regret this greatly.

The joint withdrawal of the U. S. and USSR Armed Forces in Korea,
we think, should be carried out as soon as possible from the standpoint of
principle, but the pressing question to be settled, however, does not lie
in the joint withdrawal for the following reasons:

1. Korea has been separately occupied by the two countries for
25 months. This occupation has brought great political and social confusions. These confusions will not be settled by the joint withdrawal of the
Armed Forces only, but the pending questions rather lie in how to establish
a genuine democratic provisional government, unifying North and South Korea.

2. How to stabilize public peace through the government by inducing the populace to gather around the genuine democratic ideology.

3. New Korea, which will be an independent country for the people, must be protected by the Allied Nations — America, Russia, China and
England so as to guarantee her sovereignty and freedom without threatening
of any invasion.

4. The mere joint withdrawal of the Armed Forces of the two
countries will bring about a great tragedy of the Korean people.

5. This withdrawal, furthermore, will ensure to make Korea a
military base which will bring about hostilities in the Pacific Ocean and
the Orient, judging from the forty years' experience under the Japanese
domination. If any hostilities should be openned, democracy for millions
of the young lives and billions of dollars of the national treasury would

be spent and the sublime national policy of the United States of America
through which she participated in the World War II to safeguard the world
peace, will come to naught.

I, therefore, humbly request that the preceeding terms 1 to 5
inclusive be clearly and earnestly reported by you to the Congress and
Americans. Furthermore, I hope sincerely and request that you would
raise public opinions and lead the American future policy to carry out
the project on the part of America for granting Korean independence
along to this direction through the close cooperation between America
and Russia.

Most respectfully yours,

Ahn, Chai Hong
Civil Administrator
South Korean Interim Government

- 5 -

敬愛하는 王世杰 外交部長 貴下

余는 一 東亞再建途中에서 中國外交의 重責을 맡은
貴下에게 敬意를 表하고 貴國의 蔣主席에게도
朝鮮独立援助의 最大한 國友人으로서 最大한 感謝와
最高한 敬意를 表합니다
韓國의 完全한 自主独立이 中國의 完全한 獨立에 있이
고 딸아서 東亞의 平和에 있을 것은 日本侵畧 四十年의
験에서 잘 立證됩니다. 今番 UN總会에서 韓國独立
計劃案이 따나서 美國務卿의 好意로서 上程
到한데 서울에 있는 美蘇共委, 蘇側首席代表 요
亞로 中將이 一九四八年劈頭로서 美蘇両軍同時撤退를
提案한 일은 우리 韓人은 勿論이오 唇齒輔車의 関係에

앴으 貴國中國에서로 深甚히 關心을 앋앴으 疑心을 듬니와 美蘇兩軍 同時撤退은 原則에서 … 以 韓國을 一九四五年 八、九月、美蘇兩軍이 南北으로 分斷占領한 以來 이때 二十五朔이 넘은。今日、政治的 社会的 非常히 混乱와 分裂을 招来하고。社会는 今 韓國独立計劃은 다음의 同時撤兵으로써는。解決되지 못고

(一) 이때에 南北을 統一한 眞正한 民主主義 臨時政府를 樹立한 (二) 그 政府를 中心으로 이때에 全朝鮮이 眞正 社 民主主義理念에 依하야 大衆을 集結安定케하야 公安이 確保될뿐아니라。美蘇·英·甲·等 諸聯合 國에 依하야 民族独立國家主國에서의 新朝鮮이 國際的 으로。萬一의 被侵畧의 危險없을뿐으로 一主權外 自由

民政長官室

의 保障이 確立되어야 되겠고 〔四〕 이것이 共同撤兵을

此로써 朝鮮의 民族的 悲劇을 招來할 뿐이다

〔三〕 나아가서는 口實 支配 四十年間의 經驗과 또 東亞

外 金太平洋의 戰禍를 빚을 내는 兵站基地로 함

것이 疑心없을 것입니다

貴下는 韓中親善의 許久로 世界善政의 傳統과

또는 韓國의 完全獨立이 中國의 眞正한 獨立

없는 聯關的 事情에 돌이므로 UN總會에서 如

〔一四四四四〕 諸事項에 있다 積極 主張하야 撤

韓國의 獨立完成을 極力 援助하삼 千萬仰望하나이다

余와의 사이에 同志的 信愛를 벌어 許하신즉 貴國의 為

韓總領事 劉馭萬先生에 友誼를 東亞에 를 함을

三民改長官室

貴下께 伝達하기 [illegible] 大北 [illegible] 생[illegible]

一九四七年 十月 二日

南朝鮮過渡政府民政長官

安在鴻

民政長官室

October 15, 1947

Mr. Ahn Chai Hong
Civil Administrator
South Korean Interim Government
Seoul, Korea

Dear Mr. Ahn:

Immediately upon his arrival here, Consul General Liu Yu-wan transmitted to me your letter of October 3, for which I wish to thank you. Though I have not had the pleasure of meeting you personally, I had heard a great deal about the work you are doing. I assure you that I was very pleased to receive your letter and I have read it with close attention.

The Chinese policy on Korea centres on a true and early independence of your country. You may be sure that the question of the withdrawal of the forces of the occupying powers is engaging the most serious attention of my government and on this matter I share your views.

With all good wishes,

Yours faithfully

Wang Shih-chieh

一九四七年十月十五日

安在鴻 民政長官 貴下

中華民國山X代表

王世杰

中華民國總領事 王世杰民가此地에

밝을수는 雄言할배니이다.

甘勞動 十圓 政府로, 貴國이 하
立地도 嘆이 五地와 稱之國이 되는
制暴申리에 잇홈이다. 貴國占
領軍隊撤退니 闕하아소, 中國政
右쎄가 坐호 庚戌 連호가리고, 天下同一
로, 니웃의 闕하아, 쎄가 下의 國一般
듯見호 川제니잇바이다

南朝鮮過渡政府
民政長官事務處
朝鮮, 서울

1947年 10月 17日

印度네시아共和國 大統領 스카르노閣下.

外國貿易에 關한 件.

朝鮮과 "스마트라" 及 其他國과 貿易하는 것은 兩國間의 相互 友好에 이바지할뿐아니라, 兩民族의 經濟的 活動의 發展을 爲하야도 여간 必須한 問題가 아닌 걸입니다.

朝鮮과 外國과의 貿易은, 例를들면 支那, 필립핀, 香港, 印度支那, 及 其他國間의 貿易은 最近에 이르러, 이 諸國으로하야곰 開始 된 걸이올시다. 그리고도, 우리 朝鮮航舶은 이 諸國에는 港口라도 正入港 할수있도록 承認 되여 있읍니다.

本官은 茲에 우리 朝鮮航舶이 貴國港口에 入港 할 수 있도록 容認 하여 주시기를 要請하는 바이며, 이러므로써 兩民族은 交易을 한 것이요 또 適當한 外國貿易이 이로써 始作 될 걸입니다.

本職은 茲에 宋在河氏를 紹介 합니다. 氏는 貴國에 살고 있고, 또 氏는 朝鮮과 貴國間에 交易 하는데 매우 適合人物이라고 推薦 하는 바이올시다. 이에 關한 모-든 일에 閣下 莫大한 援助를 하여 주시겠쓰면 大端히 感謝 하겠읍니다.

그리고 本職은 宋在河 以下 百余名의 朝鮮人이 貴國에서 閣下의 多大한 援助下에 無事히 歸國 함에 對하야 閣下께 感謝의 뜻을 表하는 바이올시다.

安在鴻
南朝鮮過渡政府民政長官

103

南 朝 鮮 過 渡 政 府

（美 軍 地 域）

SOUTH KOREA INTERIM GOVERNMENT

(USA ZONE)

20 October 1947

Mr. Ahn, Chai Hong,
Civil Administrator,
South Korea Interim Government,
Seoul, Korea.

Dear Mr. Ahn:

The Secretary of State requests me to inform you that your telegrams to the President of the United States, to the Secretary of State and to the Secretary of Defense, expressing condolence on the death of Major General Archer L. Lerch were received. He transmitted your message to the White House and to Mr. Forrestal.

He requested me to express to you, for the President, the Secretary of Defense and himself deep appreciation for your kind message.

Sincerely yours,

C. G. HELMICK
Brigadier General, United States Army
Acting Military Governor

—統一한 自主獨立朝鮮을 爲하야—

FOR A FREE, UNITED, INDEPENDENT KOREA

104

葛西雅 仁川石炭侵戟件

1st Nov., 1947.

Mr. E. di Garcea,
Representative,
American Securities Corp. (China).

Sir,

I have taken the liberty of approaching you because I
am sure that you would help our country.

The fact that, needless to say, the present shortage of
the materials for the re-construction of the industries is well-
known. Especially for our country we are feeling more bitterly
the shortage of the materials, and more than anything else, we
need non-anthracite coal.

We will be much obliged if you can obtain, by your esteemed
endeavours and diligences, one hundred thousand (100,000) tons
of "non-anthracite coal", no matter what is the origin of the
coal.

I remain,

Yours truly,

An Jai Hong
Civil Governor
South Korea Interim Gov'nt

SOUTH KOREAN INTERIM GOVERNMENT
Office of Civil Administraotr
Seoul, Korea

7 November 1947

Genral Gaidener, and members of the Parliament,

It is the greatest honour and pleasure for us to show our sincere-
est respect to His Majesty George VI by availing ourselves of the visit of
Lt.-General Gaidener and members of Parliament.

Under the guidance of His Majesty George VI, your Government of Labor
Party, since have come into power , has been enthusiastically doing various
efforts to emancipate weaker nations and to establish world peace.

Your great efforts amd aims are praiseworthy. At Cairo great Britain
participated in the Declaration for Korean Independence. India has been
granted her independence, and Burma is now on the verge of being granted
her independence. Not only is this fact worthy of special mention in the
history of the World, but also it is a great task to create several pages
of the greatest glory in the history of Great Britain.

In spite of the fact that Korea has already been promised her inde-
pemdemce, she is now facing great confusion and is on the verge of crum-
bling because of the division of the 38th parrallel.

We do hope your Commission will inform the world as well as your country and support our desire that through the friendship on the part of your
country and other Allied Nations a general election be held throughout North
and South Korea, a democratic, unified government be established according
to the election, the new government itself be held responsible for internal
peace, the Occupational Forces Withdraw from Korea at the same times, the
four Powers guarantee the independence and safty of Korea, and we 30 million
Koreans be united and able to establish a democratic country and participate in
safeguarding international peace.

I will try to answer any questions you may have. In conlusion may I
wish for your health and for that of the people of Great Britain.

AHN, CHAI HONG
Civil Administrator

HIS EXCELLENCY CHAIRMAN OF THE POLITICAL COUNCILS OF KOREA:-

     We, the political exiles from Formosa wish
to beg your sincere support as to the REFERENDUM we
want to ask the Peace Conference vs. Japan, and the
United Nations Organization to grant us, Formosans.
If Your Excellency considers it necessary to hear
more in details of our points of views, please send
us the permission to visit you, then we will send
our representatives over immediately.

     Very Cordially Yours,

      Thomas W. I. Liao

      Chairman, The Formosan League of

       Re-emancipation.

No.1, Knutsford Terrace,

Kimberley Road, Kowloon,

Hong Kong.

Nov. 7th, 1947.

西紀一九四七年十一月七日

香港

台灣再解放聯盟委員長　○○○

朝鮮政務委員長　閣下

我等 臺灣은 命令을 對하야 和令 威及니

國民投票에 對하야 우리가 言 國民投票에 惠澤을

救助를 要望하며 貴下의

萬君 貴下가 許諾하는 것이면 우리

要求 ... 생각하는 時는 我等의 代表를

計劃로 하여 주시와 代表를 派送

... 니다

H.B.M. Consulate-General,

Seoul.

22nd November, 1947.

Dear Mr. Ahn Chai Hong,

    Although I thanked you verbally on November 20th for your very kind and beautiful present to Her Royal Highness Princess Elizabeth on the occasion of her wedding I wish to tell you also in writing how deeply I, as the British representative in Korea, appreciate both your good wis hes to my Princess and the material expression of them.

    In accordance with your request I am taking steps to forward the gift to Her Royal Highness, who, I know, will be delighted with it.

Yours sincerely,

D.W. Kermode.
H.B.M. Consul-General.

Mr. Ahn Chai Hong,

    Civil Administrator,

        South Korean Interim Government.

SOUTH KOREAN INTERIM GOVERNMENT
Office of Civil Administrator
Seoul, Korea

25 November 1947

To : Dr. Harry B. Ansted
     ex-President , National
     University of Seoul

The task of building a new democratic education is estimable
and difficult for Korea now on the way to rehabilitation.

In the beginning of the great task Dr. Harry B. Ansted has
over come very much hardship and rendered great services to its
ground work.

The brightness of his great achievements will forever shine
over the educational history of Korea.

AHN, CHAI HONG
Civil Administrator

DEDICATED
to
Dr. Harry B. Ansted
ex-President
National University
of
SEOUL

OHN   CHAHM   KOHL   CHAL
alias
Harmony, Truth, Beauty, and Good

Harmony, truth, beauty, and good constitute the whole and are the factors of the philosophy of Korea. They are well compared to truth, good, and beauty of the Greek philosophy and can be more than them.

They will hereafter be elucidated to the world of philosophy by students Korean and foreign.

May you keep these in your commemoration note.

November in the 4280th
year of the TANGUN ERA
or November in 1947

ARN CHAI HONG

111

1948년

■ **사진_** 1948년 7월 13일. 민정장관 사임 방송 때의 민세.

2 January 1948

Mr. Ahn Jai Hong
Civil Administrator
SKIG
Seoul, Korea

Dear Mr. Ahn:

I deeply appreciate your thoughtfulness of me at
this New Year's season and express my thanks to you for
remembering me.

May 1948 bring independence and security to you
and the Korean people.

Sincerely yours,

JOHN R. HODGE
Lieutenant General, U. S. Army
Commanding

                                        12 January 1948

Honorable Ahn Chai Hong, Chairman

Korean Olympic Supporters Association

Dear Mr. Ahn:

    I want to thank you for your letter of January 7th, enclosing

a badge and one ticket issued by the Olympic Association, which I

will keep in my collection of Korean activities. It is my sincere

hope that the effort of promoting athletic sports in Korea will

continue, for all sports are healthy for the body and the spirit.

The Korean people need both health of body and sportsman spirit.

    If there is anything I can do to help your Association, please

let me know. It will be my pleasure to assist all health producing

agencies in Korea.

    Thanking you again,

                                  Very sincerely yours,

                                  Dr. Philip Jaisohn

Duk Soo Palace,
Seoul,

31 January 1948

Sir,

On 17 January, the United Nations Temporary Commission on Korea resolved to establish a Sub-Committee, to be known as Sub-Committee Two, to secure statements from Korean personalities whose views concerning the question of elections may be helpful to the Commission in the discharge of its duties.

On behalf of the Sub-Committee I now have pleasure in inviting you to discuss your views with the Sub-Committee. The Sub-Committee suggests that, if convenient to you, it should meet with you at 10.30 a.m., on Monday 2 February in the Conference Room of the United Nations Temporary Commission on Korea, at the Duk Soo Palace, Seoul.

I have the honour to be, Sir,

yours respectfully,

S.H. JACKSON,
Chairman of Sub-Committee 2

to Mr. Ahn, Chai Hong,
Civil Administrator,
South Korean Interim Government,
<u>Seoul</u>.

<u>INFO</u> <u>COPY</u>:   CIVIL ADMINISTRATOR   Prepared by:

                                             Melvin L. Alter
                                             OCA, USAMGIK
                                             APO 235 Unit 2

No Class   Routine

                                      3 February 1948

TO: State Department, Washington 25, D. C.

MGOCA______

Request following message be passed to American Ambassador to India for

Pandit Nehru, Prime Minister. "On behalf of the South Korean Interim Government,

Mister Ahn Chai Hong, Civil Administrator, and all members of the Cabinet,

wish to express the sorrow of the people of Korea over the tragic death of

Mahatma Gandhi. Mister Gandhi initiated a new phase in world history by his

opposition to aggression through a policy of non-resistance and non-violence.

The unnatural death of Mister Gandhi is not only a tragedy for the people of

India but a great loss to all mankind. Now is the time for the people of

India to bring forth a strong spirit of cooperation and unification and rely

on the strength of Mister Gandhi's teachings." End Signed Dean.

CG USAFIK   TIME IN 4 FEB 0400
                             TIME OUT " " 0910 AG
                             OCA DO

EDGAR A. J. JOHNSON   EDGAR A. J. JOHNSON
    Chief Adviser   Chief Adviser

美國 首卷中

下記電文을 初度駐屯美大使로 네주民에게 傳達하심을 바랍니다.

民政長官 安在鴻이 政府要人 一同을 南朝鮮 渡政府로 代表로서 朝鮮人이 渡美 參加 橫...에 対한 ... 表하... 非 抵抗하는 侵畧運動을 展開하...

世界歷史에 新記錄을 剝誰望음니다. 徐翁이 横... 는 大印度調에 限하야 悲慘한 事이며 ... 印度國 ... 民衆을 強力한 協調와 統一로 可能하며 世界撤하... 에 遺...

On behlaff of the South Korean Interim Government, Mr. Ahn Chai Hong,
Civil Administrator, and all members of the Cabinet, wish to express the
sorrow of the people of Korea over the tragic death of MAHATMA GANDHI. M.
Gandhi initiated a new phase in world history by his opposition to aggression through a policy of non-resistance and non-violence. The unnatural
death of M.Gandhi is not only a tragedy for the people of India but a great
loss to all mankind. Now this is the time for the people of India to be
reflected greatly, and bring forth a new spirit of cooperation and unification among themselves.

AHN CHAI HONG.

SOUTH KOREAN INTERIM GOVERNMENT
Office of Civil Administrator
Seoul, Korea.

4 Jan. 1948

Subject: Condolence Message

To   : Government of India

From   : Ahn Chai Hong
          South Korean Interim Government

We, the people of Korea are greatly startled over the tragic death of Mahatma Gandhi who developed the greatest Anti-Aggression Movement with Non-Resistance and Violence; and initiated a new record in the World History of Mankind. The unnatural death of M. Gandhi is, not only a tragedy to the people of India, but a great loss to the Mankind of the World. This is the time , for the people of India, to be reflected greatly, and bring forth a new spirit of Cooperation and Unification among themselves.

AHN CHAI HONG
Civil Administrator
South Korewn Interi Government

※ 'Jan'는 'Feb'의 오기로 추정된다.

간디 翁의 弔辭

우리 朝鮮人은 人類의 自由를 爲하야, 非暴力, 非抵抗으로 最大한 鬪爭을 展開시키어 世界史上 驚異로운 新記錄을 創作한 印度 간디 翁의 橫死를 驚愕하며 衷心哀悼한다. 그의 橫死는 印度國民의 悲慘事일뿐더러 全人類의 巨大한 損失이다. 印度의 國民은 이제 새로써 協調와 統一을 찾어 오기바란다.

一九四八年 二月 三日

南朝鮮過渡政府民政長官

改組會代表 安 在 鴻

民政長官室

國聯親團에 通牒의멧州—치 7件

6, February 1948.

Hon. Dr. K. P. S. Menon,

Chairman, The United Nations Temporary Commission On Korea,

Duk-Soo Palace, Seoul.

His Excellency;

In behalf of the Directorate of South Korea Interim Government, I have the honor to submit through you to the United Nations Temporary Commission on Korea A Message Unanimously passed by the Directorate and signed by all the Directors and myself.

With kindest regards, I am,

Respectfully yours,

Ahn Chai Hong,
Civil Administrator.

A Message

to

The U. N. Temporary Commission on Korea.

(Unanimously adopted at a special meeting of the Directorate of
South Korea Interim Government, held at 1000, 6 February 1948.)

As the ones who have participated in the government of South Korea
for two and half years, we, the Directors, are in an advantageous position
to know and to evaluate political and social conditions existing in South
Korea. For the purpose of assisting the U. N. Temporary Commission on
Korea in performing its mission charged with by the General Assembly,
we have the honor to submit to your for your consideration some of our
views on political problems that the Korean nation faces.

The Korean people did await hopefully the arrival of the U. N.
Commission. Now the attention of the whole nation is focussed on your
Commission. The multitudes of homely and patriotic folks are anxiously
awaiting the decision of the Commission. This is logical and natural.
Our nation is liberated, but it is divided into two politically and
economically by the tragic 38 degree parallel line. Undergoing political
paralysis and economic bankruptcy, we had patiently tried and waited for
two full years, but, in vain !   The U. S. - U. S. S. R. Joint Commission,
created by the Moscow Decision, had failed us after all.   However, our
national hope was revived when the General Assembly of the United Nations,
recognizing the justice of Korea, took an historical action to devise the
ways and means by which Korean national independence might be achieved.

The U. N. Temporary Commission on Korea is now here to supervise a
General Election that will lead to the establishment of a national
government of Korea. However, in discharging its mission, the Commission
confronts an insuperable obstacle in the fact that, although it is
entirely free to perform its duties in South Korea, it is prohibited
from entering into North Korea. As she did at the General Assembly of
the United Nations, Soviet Russia has persistently continued to boycott
the decision of the United Nations. And the People's Committee, a minority
dictatorial group, in North Korea faithfully abide by and support the
predetermined policy of that Nation as regards North Korea, and, in

124

fact, the whole Korea. Patriotic citizens, an overwhelming majority, in
North Korea, would, in our belief, heartly welcome the U. N. Commission.
But they could not make manifestation because the freedom of expression
is absolutely limited up there.

We believe that the Commission has reached the stage of its work
where it actually faces the dilemma whether or not it would be wise and
practicable to hold election in South Korea only. Your doubt may be
strengthened by the opinions, expounded by the minority group, that
oppose an election in South Korea only, and, further, champion a general
election in the whole Korea after the simultaneous withdrawal of both
occupation forces. However, we are of firm and frank opinion that a
general election should be immediately held in the occupation zones,
wherever it is possible to hold such an election. To make ourselves
clear to your Commission, the following reasons have to be explained at
length.

1. We desire unification, and an immediate one, too. But desire is
one thing, and reality is another. It is gratifying to read the statement
of the Commission that it does not recognize the 38 degree parallel.
However, the removal of that fatal line hence, the unification of North
and South Korea, is not to be expected, until and unless there will be
a sweeping change in the international situation, which will bring the
triumph of democracy over communism.

2. The simultaneous withdrawal of both occupation forces, at the
present juncture, without some appropriate measures for the security
of South Korea, is out of question. The barehanded South Korea will
be surely swamped by the armed forces of the North, and the map of South
Korea will be changed in red within 24 hours. So long as the Korean
people does not want the Russian system of political and social life,
they cannot afford to face such a dangerous situation   has that.
Liberated from Japanese imperialism, Korea will plunge in a hell of
human slavery.

3. South Korea has the majority right in territory and population.
Because of the mere fact that North Korea is out of our control, South

Korea itself also cannot be left in political confusion and economic

disorder. In order to achieve a real unity, and to contribute our shares

in defending the democracy of the world, our national power must be

strengthened by the establishment of a national government of Korea. That

agency alone will make the Korean nation compactly organized, economically

rehabilitated and militarily prepared.

Some friends, both foreign and Korean, cherish doubts over the

question whether the conditions in and of South Korea are such that there

could be a free and unfeltered election. Our answer to the question is

on the affirmative. So long as the leftists will not stage strikes, riots

~~and other destructive activities,~~ every and each citizen in South Korea

will be provided ^WITH a free atmosphere, in which he can cast his wise and

intelligent vote. Some of the reasons are these:

1. Having a long history of culture, the Korean people, as a whole,

possesses moral restraint, respecting others' rights.

2. Illiteracy has been greatly reduced, since our liberation, through

the carrying out of the adult education programme. Present illiteracy

is about 30 percent of the total population as compared with 70 percent

that existed before the liberation.

3. The administrative machinery of the government, central and local,

is well set up, staffed with men of efficiency and good citizenship.

4. The judiciary may not have reached as yet the standard established

in the most advanced countries. But its independence and integrity can

be ^RE lied upon to do justice to all cases brought before the court.

5. South Korean National Police is dependable for the preservation

of peace and order in South Korea. It has proved itself so. The leftists

and some superficial foreign observers have spread a false propaganda that

South Korea has become a police state. It is true that the national

police is a strong, solidified and centralized police force, somewhat

abnormal as compared with other police systems of the world. This seeming

abnormality is to be explained by the very needs of South Korea. First,

South Korea has not built up a sufficient defense forces. Secondly, national police has had to fight against the destructive activities of the communists for last two and half years. What were the tolls and what were the scope and scale of the troubles that the leftists made? Riots, 154; terroristic acts, 350; labor strikes, 229; public institutions burnt, 17; breaking jail, 3. 82 policemen were killed, and 199 civilians were murdered.

We are aware of the fact that some criticisms made against National police, based on misguided informations. But it must be remembered that National police is strong to improve itself. In order to establish democratic police methods and procedures, an ambitious educational programme is being carried. We are assured that the National police, with its present set-up, will loyally and faithfully discharge its duties that a free and unfeltered election will be carried out.

These are our best possible conclusions arrived at based on a critical analysis of the political and social conditions in Korea. You have heard the stories told by many leaders of political and social organizations, and you will hear many more. Please remember that there are all kinds of political and social organizations in South Korea, different in idealogies, strength and leadership. Without a correct evaluation and a full understanding of their history and relations, it would be impossible for the Commission to get a true picture of Korea by hearing at random. It would far more safe to hear from the common folks who are thinking nothing but the welfare of their nation.

(Signed)

7th February 1948.

Dear Mr. Ahn Chai Hong,

I write to thank you for your very kind invitation to my wife & me to dinner this evening at the Chang Duk Palace, and to tell you that to our very great regret we are unable to come since we have a visitor from Tokyo for whom we ourselves are giving a party.

Since your invitation has only just reached me I have been unable to let you

know sooner that we cannot
come. In case this letter may
not reach you in time, I have
asked Mr. Patterson to explain
& to express my regrets to you.
We are indeed sorry to be
unable to accept your very
kind invitation.

Yours sincerely,
D. W. Kermode.

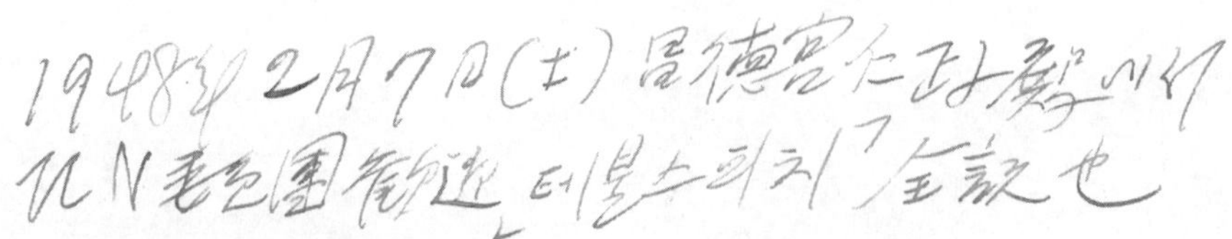

Chairman Menon and Members of the UN Temporary Commission on Korea.
Gen. Brown, and Korean and foreign dignitaries.

I esteem it great honor and am very grateful that this party is honred with so many distingished guests in spite of the cold weather and the pressure of official business.

Countries all over the world, nowa-days, are so closely connected with each other that instability of a country will have considerable influence upon the international peace. This fact, I believe, has brought the UN Temporary Commission to Korea in compliance with the decision reached at the UN General Assembly where more tahn 40 countries accentuated by the international morality agreed to aid Korea for her independence.

Korea was founded on the western coast of the Pacific over forty centuries ago. Since then she has been obliged many times to be invaded by the peoples surrounding Korea. Whenever she was invaded, however, she has desperately fought as "breakwaters" for the peace of surrounding countries as well as for her own freedom. For the past 40 years, Korea had been unfortunate enough to be enslaved by Japan, the peace of the Orient had been broken, and, accordingly, the peace of the world had been disturbed. The independence of Korea, therefore, is not only strongly longed for by the Koreans, but also a great matter of concern on the part of the countries friendly with Korea.

The UN Temporary Commission on Korea, which has taken over the great task of aiding Korean independence after the US-USSR Joint Commission had completely failed, must bring forth absolutely a good result.

Chairman Menon, I am clearly recalling your message issued on Jan 12. It is clear that there has been exchange of culture between Korea and India through central part of the Asistic Continent since several scores of centuries, I suppose, the time unrecorded in the history. The connection between these two countries is so close as preceeds. I show my great respect to India which is enthusiastically supporting the independence of Korea on the spirit of freedom and peace represented by the late Saint Maharma Gandhi who passed away a week ago.

Australia is boasting of social equality, and had fulfilled her great task during the Pacific War. It is no use for the country that I here intentionally emphasize how much the peace of the orient concerns with the country. I thank Dr. Jackson and the others of the country for their hearty kindness.

Canada had devoted herself to smash the offensive of NAZIS-Germany, and rendered great service to the Pacific War. I believe in her enthusism for Korea's independence from the standpoint of securing the peace over the Pacific. I offer my thanks to Mr. and Mrs. Patterson and the other delegates of the country for their friendship.

Korea and China has presented a joint international front over these ten conturies. They are to stand and fall together. I absolutely know that China does not regard the independence of Korea merely a foreign country's

issue. I am grateful to Dr. Liu and Dr. Hoo and the others for their
ardentness for Korea's independence.

The republic of EL-SALVADIO is famous for her love of peace and freedom, and recognizes the heart of the Koreans very well. Dr. Valle and Dr. Lindo
have come over the vast Pacific to aid Korea in acquiring her independence. I
feel secure that they are working for the Korean issue with much care. I
shook hands with them as if I had been on good terms with them for a long
time preceeding when I welcomed them in the Kimpo Air Field.

The Philiphine Islands had experienced great sacrifice in the Pacific
War, and, I believe, she is the country which knows best how much the peace
of the Orient concerned with the peace of the mankind. I believe that the
country understands the question of Korea which had fought for forty years
against Japan from the standpoint of the spirit with which they had struggled since the Spanish invasion. I miss Mr. Arranz staying now in the Philiphine Islands. I am much obliged to Dr Lung and his staff for their kind
efforts.

I suppose that Syria was composed of the same race with the Koreans
several thousands years ago, and the then Syrians spoke the language simi-
liar to Korean. I offer my infinite thanks to Dr. DJABI and his colleagues
who flew 15,000 miles from DAMASCO to let Korea obtain her independence. I do
them honor as well for their efforts to grasp the reality of Korea.

France has been the hearty friend of Korea since their revolution in
the 18th century. We highly think of their national bravery extraordinarily
demonstrated in the first and the second World War. Especially Mr. BONCOUR
has had sympathy for Korea since our exile Government was in CHUNGKING in
compliance with his country's special friendly policy toward Korea. He
came from the troublesome Balkans. I thank Mr. BONCOUR and his staff members
for their efforts as well as I expect of them very much.

On this occasion I should like to offer my thanks to Consul-General
and Mrs. Kermode of the Great Britain Empire and to Consul-General and
Mrs. Costilhes of the French Republic for their presence to this party.

It appears that an historical, important, transitional state of affairs
of a country is not easily settled. We have already observed three New Years
Days since Korea emancipated from the yoke of Japan. There, however, has
any unified, independent government established yet in Korea, which we are
longing for. Far from our expectation, international co-operation is getting worse and worse. Aggrevated keen confusion is spreading over the Balkans,
over the near East and over the Central Asia in the West. It is therefore
hardly expected that in the East an unforseen, peaceful co-operation would
bring forth the unification of North and South Korea and the establishment
of a democratic government. Under such circumstances as mentioned above,
our responsibility for adjusting the political situation, of course, can
be said great. The efforts on the part of the UN General Assembly, howver,
is far greater in the future as well as at the present.

I do and will hope, to the last moment, for the unified North and South

Korean election and the establishment of an unified government. It is quite
natural that we suppose many disturbances will occur. Whatever disturbances
of however entangled disturbances may take place, we believe and expect that
you members of the UN Temporary Commission on Korea and the Allied Powers
would completely continue your utmost for our complete independence and for
the establishment of our complete unified democratic country.

The humankind has experienced a great many things. Thanks to valuable
experiences on the part of various peoples, we can adopt for our country to
be established the strong points of the economic democracy which communism
can imply if we do not straightly adopt communism. Judging from our long
history and the objective reality of our society, a genuine democratic society which does not contain any weak point of a democratic country can be
established on the ideal of co-prosperity of the people at alrge. Of course
such a fact as preceeding lies in co-operation and efforts on our part. However, expect of you and the Allied Powers very much the completion of this
great task.

I drink to the health and success of Chairman Menon and the other members
of the Commission. Next I drink a toast for success and health of General Brown
and his colleagues.

AHN CHI HONG

REMARKS

Dr. Menon, Chairman of UN Commission to Korea, delegates, General
Hodge and distinguished guests, it is my great honor to have you come
to this party.

As we are fully aware, today, of the Nation's relations to each other
and one Nation's misfortune will make international trouble for all,
sooner or later. Therefore, United Nations Assembly has sent delegates
to Korea in order to help complete Unity and independence of Korea in
accordance some forty Nations decision which is based on international
justice.

During the period of over four thousand years of our national history of Korea,
she has been invaded by the foreign countries many times. But Korea
has been always fighting for her freedom and stands as a keystone of
peace in the Far East. Since the Japanese Imperialism took over
Korea by force, the peace of Far East as well as world peace has been
destroyed. In fact, today the independence of Korea is utmost important not only for the Korean people but also for the neighboring countries alone.

As you know the Joint Commission has failed and we Koreans have
great confidence in that you delegates will be successfull in establishing a unified, independent Korea.

Dr. Menon, Chairman UN Commission on Korea, I remember very well
your message which was broadcasted throughout the country on 12 Jan
1948. I believe India and Korea had exchanged their culture and
civilization from ancient times and we are related to each other in
many respects.

We are very sorry about the assasination of Gandhi, who is the
symbol of freedom and peace for all humanity. I am sure that the
people of India will sympathize and help the independence of Korea by
the spirit of Gandhi of India.

Dr. Jackson, the Australian delegate, you are representing one
of the greatest nations who sacrificed so much in the Pacific war
and your nation has also great interest in peace in the Pacific area.
Delegate of Canada, your country has contributed great deal in destroying Nazis Army force during the 2nd world war and has great sympathy
for the independence of Korea. Speaking about the delgate of China,
I feel like a brother because China and Korea has always common aims
in their internal and external problems. I believe that China will
consider Korean problems not only for Korea but also China's.

The delegate of El, Salvador, I have a deep appriciation for your wise suggestions and sincere attitute for the freedom of Korea.

The delegate, of the philinian Republic, your country has succeeded in obtaining complete independence very recently and I am sure that your people understand very well our situation and will do your best in helping our country.

The delegate of Syria, I believe that the culture, language and race of Syria are very simliar to that of Korea. I would like to express my deep appriciation for your participation in establishing the independnece of Korea.

Speaking about Frence, I recall the 17th century revolution of your country.

Mr. Buncour, I have heard that you have shown your sincerity and kindness to the Korean provisional government in Chungking during the war time.

May I extend my appreciation to the council generals of Great Britain and France for your coming to my party today.

Gentlemen, it seems to me that the decision of one nation's future is not so easy, as it has so much relation to the others.

When we look at the world situation, it would be passimistic rather than optimistic. Therefore, the nations who have peace and security and have more responsibility to maintain international peace and should take proper action based on Justice, immediately. That act would be the establishment of unified independence of Korea. So that the United Nations can show to the peace loving people that they are capable of maintain peace throughout the world.

Your responsibility will be the bringing of united independence of Korea, and not the establishment of separate government by all means.

We Koreans have great hope and confidence in you that you will achieve the most honorable mission.

We Koreans have much to learn from your countries and as far as we Koreans are concerned, we want to establish political and economic democratic form of government.

In order to achieve this, we need your most kind assistance and full cooperation and like wise we Koreans turn over all our hearts and loyalty in cooperating with you for succeeding Korean independence as the first symbol of carryingout the world peace.

REMARKS

Mr. Menon, Chairman of UN Commission to Korea, delegates, General Hodge and distinguished guests, it is my great honor to have you come to my part.

As we are fully aware today of the Nation's reaations to each other and one Nation's misfortune will make international trouble for all sooner or later. Therefore, United Nations Assembly has sent delegates to Korea in order to help complete Unity and independence of Korea in accordance some forty Nations decision which is based on international justice.

During the period of five thousand years national history of Korea she has been invaded by the foreign countries many times. But Korea has been always fighting for her freedom and stands as a keystone of peace in the Far East. Since the Japanese Imperialism took over Korea by force, the peace of Far East as well as world peace has been destroyed. In fact, today the independence of Korea is utmost important not only for the Korean people but also for the neighboring countries as well.

As you know the Joint Commission has failed and we Koreans have great confidence in that you delegates will be succeßsfull in establishing a unified, independent Korea.

Mr. Menon, Chairman UN Commission on Korea, I rememver vary well your message which was broadcasted throughout the country on 12 Jan 1948. I believe India and Korea had exchanged their culture and civilization from ancient times and we are related to each other in many respects.

We are very sorry about the assasination of Gandhi, who is the sumbol of freedom and peace for all humanity. I am sure that the Indian people will sympathize and help the independence of Korea by the spirit of Gandhi.

Dr. Jackson, the Australian delegate, you are representing one of the greatest nations who sacrificed som much in the Pacific war and your nation has also great interest in peace in the Pacific area. Delegat of Canada, your country has contributed great deal in destroying Nazis Army force during the 2nd world war and has great sympathy for the independence of Korea. Speaking about the delgate of China, I feel like a brother because China and Korea has always common aims in their internal and external problems. I believe that China will consider Korean problems not only Korean but also China's problems.

The delegate of El, Salvador, I have a deep appriciation for your
wise suggestions and sincere attitute for the freedom of Korea.

The delegate, of the philintana Republic, your country has succeededin
obtainingcomplete independence very recently and i am sure that your
people understand evry well our situation and will do your best in helping
our country.   *very*

The delegate of Syria, I relievathat the culture, language and race
of Syriaare very simliar to that of Korea. I would like to express my deep
appriciation for your participation in establishing the independnece of
Korea.

Speaking about France, I recall the 17th century revolution of your
country.

Mr. Bumcour, I have heard that you have shown your sincerity and kindness to the Korean provisional government in Chungking during the war time.

May I txtend my appreciation to the council general of Great Britain
and France for yoyr coming to my party today.

Gentlemen, it seems to me taht the decision of one nation's future is

not so easy as it has ao much relation to the others.

When we look at the world situation, it would be passimistic rather than
ooptimistic. Therefore,the nations who have peace and security and have more
responsibility to maintain international peace and should take proper action
based on Justice, immediately. That act would be the establishment of unified
independence of Korea.So that the United Nations can show to the peace loving people that they are capable to maintain peame throughout the world.

Your responsibility will be the bringing of united independence of Korea,
and not the establishment of separate government by all means.

We Koreans have great hope and confidence in you that you will achieve the
most honorable mission.

We Koreans have much to learn from your countries and as far as as we
Koreans are concerned, we want to establish political and economic democratic
form of government.

In order to achieve this we need your most kind assistance and full co-
operation and like wise we Koreans turn over all our hearts and loyalty in
cooperating with you for succeeding Korean independence as the first symbol
of carryingout the world peace.

TEMPORARY COMMISSION ON KOREA • COMMISSION TEMPORAIRE POUR LA CORÉE

Duk Soo Palace,

Seoul, 10 February 1948

The Secretariat of the United Nations
Temporary Commission on Korea presents its
compliments and enclose a copy of the Verbatim
Record of the meeting of Sub-Committee 2, to
which you were invited.

If you desire to correct any errors in
the record of your remarks, you are requested
to submit corrections in typewritten form to
the Secretary of Sub-Committee 2, United Nations
Temporary Commission on Korea, Duk Soo Palace,
Seoul, within forty-eight hours.

RESTRICTED

A/AC.19/SC.2/PV.13
2 February 1948

ORIGINAL: ENGLISH

UNITED NATIONS TEMPORARY COMMISSION ON KOREA

SUB-COMMITTEE 2

VERATIM RECORD OF THE THIRTEENTH MEETING

Duk Soo Palace, Seoul,

Monday, February 2, 1948, at 10:30 a.m.

Chairman: Mr. JACKSON(Australia)

CHAIRMAN: I declare the thirtheenth meeting of Sub-Committee 2 of the United Nations Temporary Commission on Korea open.

We have with us this morning Mr. Ahn Chai Hong, who is Civil Administrator for South Korea. We ant Mr. Ahn to help us to an understanding of his own office and of civil administration in South Korea in a general sor t of a way. I am sorry that we have not been able to give Mr. Ahn an opportunity to write down a few points, so that he might give us a clear statement, perhaps with some figures, but our time is short, and we shall have to deal with it in the way of a friendly chat and ask questins as they come to our minds.

Mr. AHN, Chai Hong assumed his seat. His answers and remarks were INTERPRETED FROM Korean.

Mr. Ahn Chai Hong: Although I have not written anything down on paper, I will answer whatever I know, and later, if you wish, I shall be very glad to furnish you with any information you may wish to have.

BHAIRMAN: By whom were you appointed?

Mr. AHN: In the early part of last year, at the time when I came in, there was no law prepared and no system for popular election. There, my appointment was first recommended by General Hodge to the Interim Legislative Assembly, and, thereupon the Interim Legislative Assembly appointed me Civil Administrator.

CH AIRMAN: At that time you were a member of a political party? What party was that?

Mr. AHN: It was know as the Hangkok Tok Nip. Tang- the Korean Independent Party.

CHA IRMAN: Since you have held this official administrative appointment, are you a member of a political aprty?

Mr. AHN: Later on, when they formed another political party, the Min Joo Tok Nip Tang- The Democratic Independent Party- which is not the same as the Hangkok Tok Nip Tang, they asked mo several times to take a high official position, but I refused and I am just a plain lay member of that party.

CHAIRMAN: That is your party now?

Mr. AHN: Yes.

CHAIRMAN: To whom are you responsible? Is it the Military Government or the Interim Legislative Assembly?

Mr. AHN: There are two angles. In one way, I am responsible to the Military Governor, but, on the other hand, if the Interim Legislative Assembly dislike me. then, of course, I am dimised.

CHAIRMAN: Under what law or regulations of the Military Government do you carry on ?

Mr. AHN: At the present time, in one way there is the Military Government, yet inside we have the Interim Government. Under the Civil Administrator there are different department directors and bureau chiefs and section chiefs and so on. Whatever I want to carry out, I give a message to the directors, and they carry this out. However, this has to be approved by the Military Governor.

CHAIRMAN: What departments and bureaus have you under you, and to whom do you issue instructions?

Mr. AHN: Ther are several departments under the Civil Administrator, such as agriculture, finance, justice, education, transport and communication and so on. At the same time. we have the national police department and the internal security department. These two departments are not directly responsible tp me, but there is close co-operation with them so that they carry out what I wish to suggest to them.

All the"paper work" and the governmental work is carried out by the Directors, and submitted to the Civil Administrator before messages or orders are sent out. However, there is this difficulty. My position of Civil Administrator is different from what it would be if there was an independent government where the Cabinet Chief could have the whole responsibility.

CHAIRMAN: How is the administration of these departments effected in the provinces, in the cities, and in the towns, and so on? What is the organizations for cities, provinces, municipalities and towns?

Mr. AHN: At the present time in South Korea we have nine provinces, with Seul as a "special city". The Mayor of Seoul or the provincèal governors are recommended to the Board of directors meeting, through Civil Administrator, and if thedirectors agree, then it is sent ot Military

governor; there upon the Military governor approves it and sends it to
the Interim Legislative Assembly for final approval. The executive corr-
espondence and executive work which the provincial governors and mayors
carry out are under the Civil Administrator.

CHAIRMAN: So that under you in the provinces there will be the
provincial governors, and under the provincial governors there will be
mayors, and so on. Under these conditions, is Seoul looked upon as a
"special city"; has it governor or has it a mayor?

Mr. AHN: Although the mayor of the Seoul city is the mayor he is not
completely elected by the people. He is appointed, in the same way, as
the provincial governors.

CHAIRMAN: He holds both positions—mayor and governor?

Mr. AHN: The city of Seoul is different from the ordinary city in
Western nations. In a Qestern nation the mayor has some power of controlling the police, but in Seoul the mayor has just about the same power
as the provincial governor. But it was thought that when we put the
police power under one man's control there would probably be some dis-
turbance existing in Seoul, so, therefore, we have the national police
department. At the same time, the provincial governors or the mayor of
Seoul has no power of controlling the police. However, lately we have
found it a good thing to have that very close co-operation between the
police d partment and the provincial governors in order to carry out the
work fully.

Chairman: That is going a little ahead, and answers what I was coming
to next. In the provinces there is, then, no election for the appointment
of governors; that is, no election by the people?

Mr. AHN: Of course, had we know in the beginning that this situation
would exist so long as it has done, then perhaps we would have made definite
election laws. We should have finished these things. But we have been
waiting, and waited even last year, for the Soviet and American Joint
Conference to settle such a thing, but the Conference was almost a failure.
There agian, we have been waiting for the United Nations Commission on Korea
to settle this question. However, we have drafted and acheduled these laws.

CHAIRMAN: This Sub-Committee does not wish to criticise in any way.
We are quite aware of the fact that you have been waiting, and that you

have plans to go on with these things. We are merely asking questions so
as to be informed about the position at the present time. In the provinces
the position is that the governors receive their instructions from one or
more of the Bureaus operating under the Civil Administrator?

Mr. AHN: Yes.

CHAIRMAN: When the bureaus themselves decide what is required in any
particular direction, they prepare and submit their plans to the Civil
Administrator for his approval. The Civil Administrator then recommends it to
directors meeting and if it is agrred, it is sent to the Military Governor for
approval. The bureaus then issue it to the governors. Is that correct?

Mr.AHN: The regulations written for executive work already assigned
to each provincial governor or the mayors of the cities certain responsibilities which, within his own aothority, he can carry out. He does not have
to have everythign approved every time by the Civil Administrator or the
Military Governor. However, there are several very importnat problems such as
the changing of policy or matters r garding important chaning of financial
things. Anything which is important and beyond his aouthority will be submitted
to the Civil Administrator, and thereupon the Civil Administrator, if he wishes,
will decide for himself, if it can be so decided. If he wishes to get the consent of the Military Governor, then he qill submit to the Military Governor,
thereupon final approval will be given.

CHAIRMAN: With regard to police and secunty, what do you call secruty?

MR. AHN: With regard to the Dept. of Internal Security, we call that the
Internal Security Dept. because right now this is not an independent government so we keep this dept. just for maintaining public safety and order. Therefore, so far as the name is concerned, it is one of the departments.

CHAIRMAN: The Police Departmentis responsible to the Civil Administrator
who is the complete head of the Police Department?

Mr. AHN: Of course, all the police are responsible to the Director of
the Police Department, but at the same time the Dept. Directoris responsible
to both Civil Administrator and the Military Governor.

CHAIRMAN: Who is the Department Director?

Mr. AHN: Mr. Chough, Byung OAK. However, so far his direct authority is concerned, he is directly responsible to the Military Governor. I should like to explain a little more clearly that, although we may call it a National Police, it is just like any other d partments because we gave a department director who is the top man of the National Police, and he is responsible to the Civil Administrator and also responsible to the Military Governor.

CHAIRMAN: In what way is he responsible to the Civil Administrator?

Mr. AHN: So far as hispovernmental function is concerned, of course he is under the Civil Administrator for his routine work. However, at the present time, he is not directly responsible to the Civil Administrator.

CHAIRMAN: Not in any repect at all?

Mr. AHN: In some respects. In some cases the Civil Administrator makes proposals with regard rto the general peace and order, and may have some authority to suggest to the Department Director of the National Police. However, the inside power of teh Department of Police— the changing of personnel and things like that— is strictly controlled by the Civil Administrator, but is more or less controlled by the Military Governor and occupation forces.

CHAIRMAN: As Civil Administrator you issue instructions which you may have confirmed, or have approved after they have been confirmed, and regulations which affect the whole of Korea. Now, how do you obtain the co-operation of the police to see that these regulations are carried out?

Mr. AHN: At the present time, for the good will of the people, nad for the maintenance of peace and order of South Korea, the Civil Administra-tor will suggest and tell the Director of the Police Department what to do. At the same time, in the technical part, it is not quite well un-derstood by the Department head of the National Police that whatever the Civil Administrator says must be obeyed. This is not well performed yet.

CHAIRMAN: To whom are you able to refer in cases where you are not satisfied with the cooperation you receive f om the police?

Mr. AHN: In that case, in the first place I would call the Department Director of the National Police and suggest to him and try to tell him the

importance of things, and so on. At the same time, if the Department
Director does not carry out what I wish, tehn I propose my idea to the
Military Governor and if the Militsary Governor sees fit to approve whatever
I suggest or propose, then he will tell the Police Chief to carry it out.

CHAIRMAN: You are not satisfied at the present time with the extent
of the co-operation that you receive from the Police?

Mr. AHN: At the present time, whatever I propose is not always fully
carried out, but may be some part of it will be carried out. At the same
time, the Director of the Police Department also has many wishes and many
desires to carry out, yet sometimes he might not be fully satisfied with
it himself.

CHAIRMAN: You understand we are not criticising anything. We are very
grateful for the information you are giving us, and it does not go past us.
We are not attempting to criticise; we just want to get an accurate view.

Mr. AHN: At the same time, I feel that you are here to help the Koreans
to establish a united government in this country for the will of the Korean
people. Therefore, I will try to inform you as it is and   what it is.

CHAIRMAN: We do appreciate that. In the provinces, does the same position
obtain? In other words does the governor of a province find difficulty in
getting co-operation from the police?

Mr. AHN: From time to time some of these provincial governors report
to me that there is a somewhat similar situation existing in the provinces.
However, lately we have informed them there should be much more close co-
operation, and not only close co-operation, but that the provincial police
chief should co-operate with the provincial govrnor.

From our past experience while Korea was in unrest and not quite peaceful,
we gave found that if we leave this police power to each provincial governor
then probably there will be some dabger involved by over emphasizing or over-
authorization. Therefore, we did not give too much power to the provincial
governors. But during the past two years we ahve found there are some cases
where the provincial governors should have certain powers on which to operate.

CHAIRMAN: In the city of Seoul, which is a very big area and is, as you have named it, a "special city", the police appear to be under what might ne termed an almost independent chief. That is, if we can take some of the statements we have heard s reliable.

MR.AHN: If we hold a general election the Mayor will be elected by that geheral election, and then he should have at least certain separate or independent police powers.

CHAITMAN: Would that power give him an independent force to work under his direction?

Mr. AHN: The reason I am speaking about is that if the mayor of Seoul is elected by the population, then that means that he has the confidence of the people. Therefore, if we leave some police power with him, he could utilise that power for the good of everyone in Seoul.

CHAITMAN: That would be independent of the Cheif of the National Police?

Mr. AHN: The reason that I am suggesting that the police power should be under the mayor of Seoul and, in same cases, the provincial governors, is that whenever anything happened within that province or the city of Seoul, the mayor or the provincial governor should have a certain authority to mobilize this police force inorder to stop these happenings and so on. However, on the other hand, it is also necessary to keep up the National Police as when, for instance, last year we had some trouble in the Chai Joo To province, which is an isolated island in South Korea. If it had not been for the National Police we could not have stopped these happenings, but immediately the governor informed the National Police, some policemen were flown down by aeroplane, and the happenings stopped. In that instance, if I may be allowed to speak freely, it was a happening of the leftist movement.

CHAIRMAN: At the present time, is the Seoul Police in an independent position, under which it is not entirely under the control of its national head and has no relation with the Mayor of the city?

Mr. AHN: At the present time, the police of Seoul are somewhat independent from the National Police, and at the same time, are indepedent of the mayor of the city. Is that what you mean?

CHAIRMAN: Yes.

Mr. AHN: If you will allow me to say so, I must say that you are well-informed. At the present time, in the city of Seoul we have a big area in which there are many people. Therefore we have so amny happenings going on veery day, that the police within Seoul are exercisijg their own power within their own authority.

CHAIRMAN: You suggest, with a certain amount of confidence, a police force under the mayor of Seoul. Would you suggest a similar police force or a separate force, under the governor of each province, for the same reason?

Mr. AHN: Although there is some necessity for the existing national police in order to secure khe co-operation and co-relation between the different provinces and so on whenever big things happen, nevertheless the provincial situation is just tha same as in the city of Seoul, or in any other big city where things happen. I feel that the provincial governors also should have certain privileges to control the police in order to exercise this police power under the good will of the peoples of the provinces.

CHAIRMAN: From your administrative point of view, you feel it would be proper that there should be a National Police, and that a portion of it be charged with the task of meeting national contingencies, such as the one in the South to wich you referred a short time ago. But you feel there should be other detachments-one big detachemtn for the city of Seoul and other detachmants answerable to the governors of the provinces? From an administrative point of view in general, would you consider that would be a good plan?

Mr. AHN: I fully agree with you that plan not only do I agree with it, but since the time when I becoame Civil Administrator I have been studying it, and I heartily agree with that system. Although we have nothign official, we have already planned to suggest that each provincial governor should have a certain power to utilise police power in the provinces, and, at the same time, give some instructions to the police chief in each province to very closely co-operate with the provincial governors.

CHAIRMAN: Thank you, Mr. AHN. At themoment I have nothing more to ask you, but I think the members of the Sub-Committee would like to ask some questions.

Mr. MANET: (France)(Interpretation from French) The main object of this Sub-Committee being to gether some information in order to clarify to the Commission the situation referring to the possibility of holding free elections, and since obviously the experience of Mr. AHN has led him to a knowledge of that particular aspect of the problem, I should like to ask him if he could make us benefit by that experience by throwing light on that particular rpoblem by any member of practical suggestions in that field.

MR. AHN: I will be very happy to co-operate with you. If there is time enough to permit it, I will be very happy to talk for a long time. However, if time is light, then I will be very happy to inform you in writing later on, should you so request.

Mr. Manet (France, Interpretation from French): I should like to thank Mr. AHn for his promise of co-operation. I fully realize we have very little time this morning, and that the question that I have raised is of a very general nature. I want to express again my gratitude and say how very happy we are that Mr. AHN is ready to be our disposal and allow us to benefit by his experience by allowing any of the Sub-Committee to consult him on this particular problems, and to take into consideration his suggestions and wuthorized opinion.

MR. AHN: If you request me, I will be very happy to co-operate with you whenever you like. I know your Commission is very busy, and if the Sub-Committees would like to get in touch with me, I shall be very happy to co-operate.

CHAIRMAN: There are still some members who would like to ask questions. I will call on Dr. Luna, who is an expert in his own country on administrative affairs.

Dr. LUNA(Philippine Republic): Do the provinces and cities maintain separate police organizations to maintain peace and order within their district? Is the district administration separate from the National Police? Under the present existing organization, do the provinces, the cities and municipalities maintain a separate police organization to maintain peace and order in their respective jurisdictions, independent from the National Police?

Mr. AHN: It is still operating in the direction of the National Police in each province.

Mr. WANG(CHINA: Under the present civil administration of South Korea, which government or agency or sub-division, if any, is charged with the administrative details of the registration of votors?

MR.AHN: During the last period we appointed what is know as an Election Committee composed of 15 pe sons. These persons from every direction, some leading political parties, and at the same time, even though they are members of a certain organization or party, we tried to make it so thatthey were fair-minded persons. However, at the same time we tried to push along some more detail work which would be helhful to the popular election. Nevertheless, when I submitted that plan to the Military Governor, the Military Governor felt that he would not wish to interfere in any sort of way with the United ations Commission because it was their job to set up and direct and decide how the popular election should be held. Therefore, we did not fully carry out that programme; yet there is already a Committee appointed. The detailed form of the law might be helpful for the general election. If the United Nations Commission wish to see these things for their own reference, they may do so. At the same time, the Commission has a full chance to carry out whatever it wishes.

Mr. PATTERSON(CHANADA): May I interject a question on this last point? Was thiseplan to which Mr. AHN has referred prepared after it was known that the United Nations Commission was to be appointed, or wasitoabplan for an election which was envisaged before the Commission was appointed?

Mr. AHN: It was really on the occasion when the Joint-Commission- that is, American and the Soviet Union-met, last year to set up an independent democratic government of Korea. At that time, the Interim Legislative Assembly members felt that the Joint Commission would decide to set up a certain from of government and they would probably need something to refer to. Therefore the Assembly members drafted this and of ciurse, submitted it to the Military Governor, but the Military Governor did not act upon that programme, because it was the job of the United Nations Commission, and we might as well wait until they come, and whatever the United Nations Commission plans we will follow.

At the same time, although we appointed 15 members of the Election Commission in the central district, we have not yet established any branches of the local election committees.

DR. DJABI(SYRIA): There has been on election in South Korea, why cannot a government be formed from the Interim Legisaltive Asxembly'

MR.AHN: As you will perhaps know, at the present time we have here what is known as the Interim Legisaltive Assembly of South Korea, but it is pretty hard to say it is fully representative of both North and South Korea. Last year, when we had the Soviet and American Joint Commission, we thought that soon a new government would be formed and there would be an election in both Nroth and South Korea. We are still waiting and waiting for what we hope to see- a democratic united government in both North and South Korea. Some people think that we should hold an election and form a government for South Korea alone, but we hope to see both North and South hold a general election and form a national assembly.

Another thing I wish to add is that at the present time we have 90 members in the Interim Legislative Asxembly, half of them elected members and half of them appointed by the Military Governor. Mostly, these appointed members are leaders who came from Manchuria or China or other places, where they were Korean patriots, and they are also mostly of the political parties and other groups.

Mr. MANET(FRANCE)(INTERPRETATION from French): If I understand correctly the answer given by Mr. AHN to the question put to him by the representative of Syria, the Interim Legislative Assembly did not form a government because that was not the purpose for which that body was created, the purpose for its creation being the drafting and implementation of a certain number of laws and of an administrative machine.

Mr. AHN: Then we see the condition as it is now in the Interim Legislative Assembly, we know that what the French representative ahd just said is true. On the other hand, when the Interim Legislative Assembly was established, it was to carryout not only what the French representative has stated, but also we try and get both leftists and rightists together and try to carry out the programme of the Joint Commission smoothly, and so on. However, the result of the second Joint Commission last year did not bring any good result, therefore,at the present time, the only work left to the Interim Legislative Assembly is executive work and the drafting of ordinances and laws or other matters which are more concerned with executive orders.

CHAIRMAN: I think you were imprisoned by the Japanese for two years?

Mr. AHN: If all the dates are counted, I was in prison almost eight years. I was in gaol altogether nine times, sometimes only for ten days and other times for months and years.

CHAIRMAN: I think that under these conditions you have quite a clear opinion of the Japanese domination, I can say that I know a lot about these things. I feel I was one of the Korean patriots who tried to move on to a better government.

CHAIRMAN: I do not think we will ask any more questions. I must say that we are very hopeful that at least your patriotic self-sacrifice amy be rewarded very soon, and that you will be able to get an independent government for Korea very soon.

Mr. AHN: I appreciate very much your co-operation towards the establishment of an independent government in Krea.

The meeting rose at 12.10 p.m.

SOUTH KOREAN INTERIM GOVERNMENT
Office of Civil Administrater
Seoul, Korea

6 March 1948

Subject: A recommendation for Police Reorganization from KUNSAN
Special Branch of the Korean Independence Party

To   : Maj. Gen. William F Dean
Military Governer

Dr. Edgar A J Johnson
Chief Adviser to Government

1.   Following is the translation of a recommendation submitted
to the Office of Civil Administrator by Mr. YOON SUK KOO, Chairman of
the KUNSAN Special Branch of the Korean Independence Party for a complete reorganization of the National Police.

25 February 1948

 Recommendation

(1) Demanded the present National Police be entirely reorganized.

(2) The ground for our demand is as follows.
(A) In a democratic country, the police should exist for the
people, but not for the police themselves. In no way,
furthermore, the police cannot be for a party, nor a
group.
(B) In spite of this stern fact, the present Korean National
Police, judging from a strictly just point of view, is
far worse than that of under Japanese Domination in which
the colonial police had been proud of their "omnipotence"
for 36 years. To make matter worse, the present National
Police are so much prejudiced that the police appear to
exist for a certain, single party or a group.
(C) Since the liberation of Korea, the people have unanimosly
called for a democratic police while the Government also
have been doing its utmost for the realization of the
police requested, but the result has proved quite contrary.
The most leading factors having brought forth this worst
result are two:

Those who had served in the police under Japanese Domination, and faithfully worked for Japan while tor-
turing Koreans, are again employed in the present
police as leading staffs.

The supreme leaders of the present police consist

151

sorely of personalities from a certain political party.

It is, therefore, no exaggeration to say that the present
Korean National Police have succeeded to the attitude of the
Japanese oppressive and threatening police; accordingly the
people at large have been obriged to continue the disgusting
antipathy toward the present police. The people have thus
alienated from the police. It is easily proved by the fact
that the various riots, since the emancipation of Korea, have
taken place chiefly and ever against the police. It is also
clear that a certain political party has made the most of
the police of which the supreme leaders consist of leading
persons from the party in enlarging and strengthening the
party influence.

(B) It is indispensable for Korea to establish a democratic
police in the stage of her national construction. Moreover,
it is far essential for the coming general election in *free and peaceful* atmosphere under the supervision of the UN Korean Commission that
the National Police should be entirely reformed. Such per-
functory reform as verbal or documentary will not bring
about a free atmosphere by any means.

/s/ YOON SUK KOO
Executive Chairman,
KUNSAN Special Branch of the
Korean Independence party,
KUNSAN City

2.   This recommendation is hereby submitted to you for your information and consideration.

AHN CHAI HONG
Civil Administrator

Seoul.

8th March 1948.

Dear Mr. Ahn,

Many thanks for your letter of the 17th February forwarding a copy of your delightful speech at the banquet which you so kindly gave us in our honour. We shall cherish the pleasant recollections of the banquet as well as the kind sentiments expressed by you.

Yours sincerely,

Ahn Chay Hong, Esq.,
   Civil Administrator,
      Seoul.

HEADQUARTERS XXIV CORPS
Office of Deputy Commanding General
Seoul, Korea

9 March 1948

Mr. and Mrs. Ahn Chai Hong
Seoul, Korea

Dear Mr. and Mrs. Ahn:

Recent orders from the War Department transfer me
to Washington D. C. I regret that I am not able to remain
in Korea to see the day when your urgent and justifiable
desire for union and independence is realized.

It has been a great pleasure for me to have known
you and so many of your able countrymen. I have enjoyed
the fine contact with you. My thoughts remain with you and
I will continue to wish as urgently as do you for union and
independence for all Korea.

Mrs. Brown joins me in best wishes and goodbye.

Sincerely yours,

ALBERT E. BROWN
Major General, U. S. Army
Deputy Commander

18 March 1948

TO : Lieutenant General Hodge, Commanding General, USAFIK.
       Major General Dean, Military Governor, USAMGIK.
       Major General Helmick, Deputy Military Governor, USAMGIK.
       Dr. Johnson, Chief Advisor, USAMGIK.

FROM: Ahn Chai Hong, Civil Administrator.

May I submit to you the following statement for your reference in helping Korea gain her independence as well as good for Korean people themselves?

In the past several times I have submitted to you my desires and plans by oral and written statement. However my honest statements were not conveyed properly to you and some misunderstanding which which was quite contrary what I wanted to express to you, has occured.

I trust present statement would be conveyed to you in a right way.

SUBJECT: Regarding Mr. Kim Koo and his treatment.

In my humble opinion, the right or proper treatment of Mr. Kim Koo is very important in analyzing the following two respects in the time of reconstruction of Korea and American assistance for Korean independence.

I. Regarding assassination of Chang Duk Soo and its background.
From the end of year of 1945, whenever the political leader was attacked or assassinated, some political leaders and political parties were suspected as related with the assassination. Since the Anti-trustship demonstration on 23 of June in 1947, Mr. Kim Koo was the person in question whether he is the man to be arrested or not, and he was called to the Military Court on 12 of March in 1948 for the purpose of witness.
It might be possible that Mr. Kim may be involved in Mr. Chang's case, and even some kind of sanction would be applied to him.
Concerning this matter, I would like to emphasize the fact that Mr. Kim should be completely released from the Mr. Chang's case for

the purpose of Korean-American high policy.
The reasons for Mr. Kim's complete release
is as follows:

(1) Before the military court, Mr. Kim Koo himself has formly denied the fact that he has
any relation with the case.

(2) The defendant themselves have also testified that Mr. Kim Koo did not issue any
order to assassinate Mr. Chang Duk Soo.

(3) Such two facts show that legal basis to
apply to Mr. Kim Koo is not enough.

(4) In a judgement of the present circumstance, Mr. Kim Koo's party shall be
considered as an extreme rightest, but
this definition will not apply to the
party as a whole.

(5) It is true that when assassination of
political leader has occured, the
followers of Kim Koo were suspected, but
the general public is fully aware that there is
some other groups or party which more ag-
itates and lead such murder cases.

(6) There will a danger of Anti-American
feeling of the general public, because of
that Mr. Kim Koo's party alone is responsible
for agitation of assassination and this policy
is not right in political point of view.

(7) At the present time, Mr. Kim Koo is making
progress for realization of unification of
South and North Korea.

(8) Mr. Kim Koo is opposing South Korean election
and he is taking an attitude of uncompromise
with USAMGIK. Therefore, if Mr. Kim Koo is
subject to apply any kind of sanction for Mr.
Chang's assassination case, the general public
will be misleaded to the direction of Anti-
American feeling, because they, (general
public), think that Mr. Kim's sanction is based
on uncompromise attitude with American policy
rather than Chang's case.

Accordance with before mentioned facts, it would be the
most desirable to completely release Mr. Kim Koo from the Mr.

3

Chang's case will make elemination of political leader's
assassination in the future.

It would be worth while to maintain political power
balance in using such opposite power when a country has
political relation with another race.

II. Regarding Mr. Kim Koo's plan of the South and
North Korean political leader's meeting.

At the present time the realization of such meeting is almost impossible. The compromise policy between
the United States of America and Soviet Union has broken
and Soviet Union refused permission of UN entrance into
North Korea. In this fact such meeting would be very difficulty. As long as UN provides such meeting, the Soviet
Union will definitely refuse it, and when she notices that
the United States of America backs such meeting, she (Soviet
Union), will suspect of the U.S. political intention. Even
South and North Korea unification conference is formed,
it would be the question have the relations between U.S. and
Soviet Union will be developed.

If U.S. provides South and North unification conference in accordance with Kim Koo's plan, whose followers
oppose the American military policy and has public attention concerning before mentioned Chang's case, it would be
very effective. This kind of work should be handled through
General Hodge in sending a official letter to Soviet Union
Commanding General in North Korea.

General Hodge's work would be just to transmit Mr.
Kim Koo and other leader's wishes and desires, and let them
decide the final matter.

The U.S. Government will not need to take too much
consideration to the final outcome of the conference. If
Mr. Kim Koo and his followers fail in the conference, then
the U.S. Government will have something to say to them.

The word and action of Mr. Kim Koo and his followers will cause great excitment to the public and U.S. Government attitude toward him and his followers will give great
influence to the relationship between Korea and the United
States of America.

Realizing this fact, I believe your most careful
consideration about my humble recommendation is very urgent.

Very sincerely yours,

Ahn Chai Hong
Civil Administrator.

20 March 1948

TO: South Korea Interim Government
     Seoul, Korea

     Civil Administrator
     All Members of Cabinet

     'On behalf of my colleagues and myself I wish to
convey to you the expression of our sincere gratitude for your
message of sympathy in the irreparable loss that India has
sustained by Mahatma Gandi's death. He was, indeed, a world
figure of profound moral influence. Though his death is universally
mourned in India, the people of this country are determined to
persevere in the path of unity, peace and good will, along which he
was leading us.'

                         PANDIT NEHRU

FB/MK152 TOKYO 35 VIA RCA 19 70S/

NLT AN CHAIHONG CIVIL ADMINISTRATOR

  SEOUL

KINDLY ACCEPT AND CONVEY TO YOUR COLLEAGUES IN INTERIM

GOVERNMENT MY SINCERE THANKS FOR ALL THEIR COURTESIES AND

KINDNESS STOP BEST WISHES FOR EARLY ATTAINMENT OF KOREAN

INDEPENDENCE

  MENON

Form 112 Z-TD 89

SOUTH KOREAN INTERIM GOVERNMENT
Seoul, Korea

21 March 1948

Memorandum for

South Korea is standing on the verge of a grave danger. The people
in general are in opposition to the military government. This is especially so in the regions of Korea which can truly be called the "grainary
of Korea". If this opposition of the people becomes violent during the
farming seasons, it will completely undermine the food production program and
will then endanger the whole administration of the government.

A certain department in the government, cooperating with certain
groups, is intentionally ignoring this critical situation, declaring that
it is all caused by the "plotting of destructive elements". This accusation
is too simple, but by it, these people intend to justify their present
activities and maintain the status quo.

Needless to say, the present situation requires careful study and
consideration. Experience gained in my present capacity for more than
a year and a half convinced me that I should make the above statement.

Prompted by my sense of duty, I take the liberty of committing myself to the following suggestions:

I Elections and the Social Situation

A. Once the American Military Government in South Korea has determined
to hold elections in accordance with the resolution of the United Nations
Little Assembly, we must try to obtain the best possible results; to promote the prestige of the government; and to restore the morale of the people
so that they will be economically and culturally productive. Only then
can we have political and social stability and progress. On the other
hand, should the elections turn out to be unworthy of the name, South
Korea will be thrown into an intolerable situation. Thus we are com-
pelled to scrutinize and take stock of the present situation in South
Korea.

B. It is unnecessary to reiterate all phases of conditions prevailing
in South Korea. Suffice it to say that the main causes of the unfortunate
situation are: (a) the trend of world affairs which are beyond the control of any one nation, and which are particularly beyond that of such
a weak nation as Korea, (b) occupation of Korea by two hostile powers,
(c) political collapse of the former regime, (d) social upheaval of the
Korean people, (e) industrial and economic dislocation of Korea, (f)
inability of speeding readjustment to the new situation, (g) mass ignorance of the causes of unfavorable conditions and the means of improving

them, (h) misconduct of party politicians, (i) maladministration of the
government as a whole and particularly of certain of its sections.

Confronted with these difficulties, no administrator, however able,
can satisfy the peoples' needs and desires, and gain their full confidence and support. To speak the truth, the people are becoming increa-
singly dissatisfied with all sections of the government -- that is, its
administration, justice, and police. This is most striking in the case
of the police, and it is not difficult to analyze the causes of this
growing discontent.

The police are in charge of maintaining peace and order; they are
in more direct contact with the people; the scope of their activity is
broader. Hence the police have become the symbol for the people's resentment and opposition. Even more, by having become the criterion for
judgement of the government in general, the police have clouded or nul-
lified the progress and positive accomplishments of other departments.

C. The estrangement between the people and the government, as described above, and especially the dangerous antagonism between the police
and the people, is to a certain extent the result of inevitable objective conditions. But what has made the matter particularly dangerous
is that the extreme leftists, including the South Korea Labor Party have
been utilizing an internally aggravated and growing popular opposition to
the government for their own political advantage.

No one can deny that the former People's Committees, organized in
South Korea immediately after the liberation, had strong and enthusiastic
nation-wide support. The police were determined to extirpate them.
They took a strong "might makes right" policy, that is one of active use
of force and oppression to gain their ends. In cooperation with political parties and social organizations, the police launched a wild hunt
for leftists. Arrests and tortures raged; terrorism was rampant. And as
this situation progressed, it became clear that extreme rightists and
unscrupulous adventurers had entirely taken over the police. At last,
instead of standing as the guardian of a legal state, representing law
and order, the police turned into an organization controlled by certain
political parties and cliques.

Certainly, at times, a government needs a strong hand, particularly
when faced with an uncompromising, rebellious minority. But naked force
only breeds force, so the following requires careful consideration:

First, the only effective way of combatting communists is not to
resort to the fascistic tactics of violence, but to stand up firmly for

democracy, law, and order. Now that the power of the police is in the
hands of a certain party and the extreme rightists, the strife between
leftists and the police is not one between law and violence, but one
between communists and fascists.

Second, since the police have been taken over by a small clique of
extreme rightists, they repel every shade of liberalism and democracy.
They have suppressed liberals, democrats, and even extreme rightists who
are not of their mind, labelling them as "leftists" or "reds".

Third, having driven leftists underground and having silenced all
liberals and democrats, the police are now going as far as to even
suppress and exploit the defenseless little common man. They have
snuffed out the spontaneous will of the people; they have stifled democratic tendencies; they are now a symbol of corruption and oppression.
No wonder that the police have become the object of hatred, resentment,
and opposition of the people.

We all realize that we are facing an epoch-making period in the
history of Korea, and that we are standing at the cross-roads of life
or death. We must succeed in the elections. The elections must be
free, must be participated in and supported by the majority of the
people. If things remain as they are, I dare say the elections are
doomed to failure. The main reason is that South Korea is not free
and is unfit for elections, largely because of the suppression, law-
lessness, and corruption of the police. It is therefore imperative
that we should completely regenerate and reform the police.

II Reform of the Police

The police should be so changed that the people shall be able:

(1) to enjoy freedom and security
(2) to trust in the police and feel they receive justice and
    protection from them
(3) to be friendly and cooperative with the police

What is wrong with the present police is not the system but the
personnel composing it. Therefore thepolice personnel in pivotal
positions must be reexamined and incompetent and unsuitable persons
should be promptly and unhesitatingly removed from office. They should
be replaced by men of character, integrity, and ability, and preferably
by those who have experience in police service, regardless of whether
they served under the military government or the former Japanese
Government.

Since this change is a matter of great importance, it is fraught
with danger if unscrupulously used towards private or political ends,
and so it must be planned in secret and executed with speed.

-3-

162

Considering the present situation, persons in the higher positions
in the police divisions, including chiefs, must be replaced, preferably from
inspectors. Persons in higher positions in "gun" and "pu" police stations,
including their chiefs, must be discharged or removed.

III Social and Political Education of the Masses

Factors which are conditioning present-day Korea have been enumerated
above, and restated, there are two general groups of influencing conditions,
one beyond the control of Korea, and the other within her power to change
and direct. The latter group, of which Koreans must be fully aware, are:
(a) maladministration, (b) mass ignorance of the means of improving unfavorable conditions, (c) lack of clearly defined goals, with the resul-
tant hesitancy to enlist the full strength of the people in a vital program of reconstruction and rebuilding.

While a reform of the police will remove one of the fundamental causes of maladministration and resentment against the government, unless
a positive program is instituted to eliminate mass-ignorance, the people
will be unable to avail themselves of the benefits of improved conditions.

In education nothing is more important than motivation, and so for
a people, nothing is more important than understanding the meaning of
elections. On the eve of this great occasion, we should inform the people
to the full extent of what they should know about the duties and responsibilities of a citizen in an election. And we should insist that they be thoroughly familiar with the rules and regulations governing the elections, as
well as with the machinery by means of which an election is carried out.

Since a free election is an outstanding symbol of democracy, this is
an opportunity to teach the people the necessity for working together,
building greater economic self-sufficiency, selecting wise and capable
leaders, and seeking compromise without resort to force and within the
bounds of law.

I would like to suggest that we select able, well-informed, and
trustworthy representatives from among the common people who will carry
on an educational campaign in order to encourage the understanding of
these ideas, stressing particularly the following points:

(1) Efforts at democratization by the military government, including
the recent land reform laws, dissolution of the New Korea Company, and the
significance of Public Law No. 176.
(2) Governmental efforts for industrial rehabilitation including
importation of fertilizers and essential machinery.
(3) The importance of a democratic government in South Korea as
a sound possible basis for unification of North and South Korea.
(4) The concept of "one party, one state" is totalitarian and can
only lead to violence and resulting permanent division of Korea.

-4-

(5) "The secret of justice is in the courage to defend it". The misguided energies of private force organizations must be redirected and compulsory donations must be stopped. Cases of intimidation and any other breach of the election laws should be reported to appropriate authorities, and notorious profiteers should be exposed.

(6) Those disseminating the educational program should feel free to call on such civil organizations which are impartial, trustworthy, and in high esteem with the people for support.

In short, the people should know and feel that all their efforts for elections, the national assembly and the government are part of the grand purpose of establishing a unified, democratic, and independent Korea.

23 March 1948

SUBJECT: Resignation.

TO   : Lieutenant General John R. Hodge, Commanding Gene-
ral USAFIK.
Major General Dean, Military Govenor, USAMGIK.
Major General Helmick, Deputy Military Governor.
Dr. Johnson, Chief Advisor, USAMGIK.

I have accepted Civil Administrator's position of
South Korean Interim Government, in accordance with the rec-
commendation of General John R. Hodge, Commanding General,
United States Army forces in South Korea, because of my firm
belief that cooperation with the American Military Government
policy based on transforming of an administrative authority
from the american personnel to the Korean personnel, would be
right and proper direction in achieving unification of North
and South Korea by the assistance of the United States of
America, Soviet Union and other United Nations and reconstruction of economic system for the purpose of solving livelihood and establishment of democratic government by the
Korean people themselves.

During the period of more than one year, cooperation policy between the United States of America and Soviet
Union has broken, and one of my important political beliefs
which is unification of leftist and rightiest, has also
failed. At the same time, political confusion and problems
of livelihood, are getting worse, and it would be very difficult to achieve my expected original aim. Therefore, I
feel that I am not able to continue my present position as
Civil Administrator in SKIG. Moreover, in accordance with
the Interim Committee, UN, the United Nations temporary
Commission on Korea will observe general election in as much
of Korea as is accessible to it, and it is a time to change
Civil Administrator who is supporting UN decision heartfully
and has same political belief which is that of the UN. Hereby I submit my resignation as Civil Administrator in South
Korea Interim Government.

During the my tenure of Civil Administrator, there
were many criticisms and oppositions regarding my political
beliefs, and other points of views, and still some points
have not cleared, but as far as I am concerned, my conscience
is clear and I am not ashamed of myself. Regarding this
matter, I would like to express my deep appreciation for your

unchangeable trust upon me.

I feel sorry to leave my position in the time of critical period in Korea, but as I before mentioned, it is the time to have an able man in the Civil Administrator's office as soon as possible.

I sincerely hope that you will accept my resignation of Civil Administrator SFIK.

Sincerely yours,

Ahan Chai Hong
Civil Administrator, SFIK.

HEADQUARTERS
UNITED STATES ARMY MILITARY GOVERNMENT IN KOREA
Office of the Korean Affairs Advisor
to the Military Governor
APO 235   Unit 2

2 April 1948

Mr. Ahn Chai Hong
Civil Administrator
Capitol Building
Seoul, Korea

Dear Mr. Ahn:

This office has been asked to inform you that due to a mishandling of an invitation sent to you by Mr. J. E. Jacobs, U. S. Political Advisor, to his party held on Sunday, 28 March, your invitation was, unfortunately, misplaced. This omission was not discovered until the following Monday at which time it was too late to rectify the mistake.

We sincerely regret that this special invitation failed to reach you.

Sincerely,

R. S. WATTS
Korean Affairs Advisor

SOUTH KOREAN INTERIM GOVERNMENT
Office of Civil Administrator
Seoul, Korea

12 April 1948

Mr. D. SINGH
Chairman
UN Temporary Commission On Korea

Dear Mr. Singh;

I have the honour to introduce to you and members of your Commission several members of the Association For Democratic Free Election, which is, I can avow, composed of really democratic, progressive personages from legal and acadamic circles.

These personages have been making various efforts to hold the coming general election absolutely freely. and to avoid unfree election. Furthermore they are doing their utmost to elect as many patriotic and progressive persons as possible by preventing abstention from voting, and from standing as candidates so as to avoid a party's monopolization of the election.

In this point of view, I do hope that you assist them as friendly as possible after having interviewed them. To accomplish the mission of holding a free general election I have still been staying in my position.

Doing you honour and anticipating your kindness,

Respectfully yours,

AHN CHAI HONG
Civil Administrator

朝鮮駐屯 美軍政府本部

10 May 1948

一九四八年 五月 十日

Mr. Ahn, Chai Hong
Civil Administrator
South Korea Interim Government
Seoul, Korea

南朝鮮過渡政府
民 政 長 官
安 在 鴻

Dear Mr. Ahn:

Justice reports that the trial of Cho Chung Ha and Cho Soong

司法部는 報告하기를 趙晶夏 及 趙順九의 審理

Koo will be held shortly after the elections.

는 選擧卽後 開始될 것이라고 합니다.

The number of witnesses, amount of testimony, and duties of

證人의 數爻, 證言의 分量, 選擧에 關係

the judge in connection with the election have all caused delay

한 審判官의 職務等, 이모든 것으로 因하야 被告

in bringing the defendants to trial.

들의 審理가 遷延 되었읍니다.

C. G. HELMICK
Major General, United States Army
Deputy Military Governor

美國陸軍少將
副軍政長官   씨·지·헐믹

南朝鮮過渡政府의 樹立과
第三党組織의 浪藉.

吳政光官

安在鴻

一九四八年 〇月 〇日

國會議員 選擧

이같이 外地 教育을 받은 軍政의 官吏들이 中心으로 第三政黨을 組織코
後에 議員으로 中心으로 第三政黨을 組織코
또 新政權에 参加코자 計画을 하고 있는
또 新政權에 参加코자 하였으나 計画은
第三政黨이 政治舞臺에 登場케 되리라는 推測도 不難
會議에 揭載되리라 政治舞臺에 登場케 되리라는 推測도
이 念願을 받어 新政黨을 …
이 勢力이 … 官界에 發身한 者들이라
… 더욱 其邊의 …
… 組織으로써 現段階의 時局을 支持擁護
…… 方面에서 …로 組織時에 ……
…… 大部分 ……
… 綜驗을 材料로 하였으니 새…으로 …對策을

本信은 別本을 鞄送]

Lt. Gen. John R. Hodge
Commanding, USAFIK

15

13 May 1948

My dear General Hodge!

    I greet you with all my heart. The success in the General
Election carried on the 10th of May will surely lay a foundation
for the initiation of New Establishment, not only within the
country but as well as internationally, and I sincerely congratulate you for this.

    I have written a book entitled "Ancient History of Korea" de-
riving my time when I was in prison or at home in the country
village under the Japanese severe oppression. It was written, line
by line, in the spirit of independent movement woven my heart and
seoul into it when failed in Independent Movement.

    I have the honour to offer you who are rendering so great a
help to the completion of our independence, a copy of this book and
beg you to accept it and keep it as an eternal souvenir although
you may not read the same.

                        Respectfully Yours,

                        AHN CHAI HONG
                        Civil Administrator

Office of U.S. Political Adviser
Seoul, Korea
May 17, 1948

Mr. Ahn Chai Hong
Civil Administrator
South Korean Interim Government
Seoul

Dear Mr. Ahn:

With reference to radio transmitted April 20, 1948 on your behalf to the Secretary of Foreign Affairs of the Philippine Republic through the American Embassy at Manila, expressing regret and condolences on the death of President Roxas, we have now received from the Embassy the enclosed copy of note dated April 30, 1948 from the Department of Foreign Affairs of the Republic of the Philippines, expressing the appreciation of their Government for your message.

Sincerely yours,

Joseph E. Jacobs
United States Political Adviser

Enclosure:
    Note.

西紀一九四八年五月十七日

美國政治顧問으로서 E.짜코스

南朝鮮過渡政府

民政長官 安在鴻 座下

一九四八年四月二十四日에 貴下를 爲하야 [illegible]

此件을 貴大統領閣下에 比擬하야 書面으로

[illegible]電으로써 此를 住在美國大使로써 通知코 比律

賓外務部에 記電으로 傳達되엇으[illegible] 四月三十

[illegible]에 附한 此律賓外務部意에 此別後에 慶禮

이 書輔이 美國大使로써 [illegible] 三船車見君

少將外

The Department of Foreign Affairs presents its compliments

to the United States Embassy and has the honor to acknowlege

the receipt of its note (1261) of April 21, 1948, regarding the

receipt of a telegram dated April 20, 1948, from the American

Political Adviser at Seoul conveying a message of condolence

over the death of President Manuel Roxas from Ahn Chia Hong,

Civil Administrator, South Korean Interim Government. It will

be appreciated if the Embassy can transmit to the Civil Adminis-

trator and the members of his Cabinet, the appreciation of this

Government for their expression of regret and condolence.

Manila, April 30, 1948

ASPA-FM-jbc

西紀一九四八年 四月三十日

外務部에서는 美國大使에게 致謝를 [illegible]
一九四八年四月二十五日에 在朝鮮美國政府 政治顧問
[二五]에 南朝鮮過渡政府 民政長官 安在鴻이
此에 大統領으로부터 [illegible] 並 [illegible] 에 對하
電(一三六二)號으로써 對하야 [illegible]한데 美國
大使가 政府에 [illegible] 亞洲에서 [illegible] 弔詞에 對하 感
謝를 [illegible] 民政長官 安在鴻이
以感謝希望 [illegible] 傳達되 [illegible] 感謝
이다

HEADQUARTERS XXIV CORPS
Office of the Commanding General

APO 235
SEOUL, KOREA

19 May 1948

Mr. Ahn Chai Hong
Civil Administrator
South Korean Interim Government
Seoul, Korea

Dear Mr. Ahn:

I have just received your letter of 15 May and the "Ancient History of Korea" accompanying it. I appreciate both the letter and the book more than words will express.

In my opinion the results of the General Election have tremendous significance. Not only do they offer the Korean people a new era, but they are a complete vindication of democratic processes over Communism, where the "Free Atmosphere" gave the Communists and misguided dissident groups full opportunity to persuade the people away from the elections.

The confidence of the United States in the sound judgment of the good people of South Korea has been completely justified.

Thank you again for your thoughtfulness and with all best wishes for your continued good health and success, I am,

Sincerely yours,

JOHN R. HODGE
Lieutenant General, U. S. Army
Commanding

176

To: Lt. Gen. John R. Hodge,   June 1 1948
       Commanding General, USAFIK
                Subject: Resignation
From: Ahn Chai Hong, Civil Administrator

Dear Sir,

I hereby submit my resignation to you as civil administrator
of South Korean Interim Government, believing this is a proper
time to do so.

As you are fully aware I have accepted the position of civil
administrator due to the delay of establishment of united Korean
government, and American policy toward Korea was transfer of administrative authority from American personnel to Koreans personnel
as was announed by General Hodge in the first part of 1947 as a
means of achieving establishment of Korean independent government.

In accordance with the transfer of executive athority, I accepted the most important position by the recommendation of General
Hodge for the purpose of solving the difficult probles such as
personnel changes, police, food and pro-Japanese collaborators problem, etc.

In the past, I have tried to accomplish the abovementioned problems by smoother method that what the general public have expected,
but I did not succeed because of various unexpected obstacles and
restrictions.

The second US-Soviet joint conference whith was held from the
last part of May 1947 in order to achieve unified Korean government
has failed and my main political belief--unification of leftist and
rightist groups--has become weak by the obstacles of international
politics. Therefore, my opponent political power is getting strong-
er and political democratization based on governmental official
changes and unification of leftist and rightist groups has complet-
elyfailed. I regret and blame myself for the fact that I did not
submit my resignation immediately at that time. It is also my great
regret that coming of the United Nations Temporary Commission on
Korea and decision of the general election in South Korea under the
observation of UN have forced me to delay my resignation.

I am not trying to defend myself that my resignation is
based on what General Hodge said to me"to be patient with clear
conscience." In my political moral point of view I thought that some
one who supports the general election in that part of Korea which is
accessible heartily should be entitled to such an important position
as civil administrator, but my resignation would bave been recognized as opposition to south Korean election, and I have waited
until the general election is over considering the importance of
international relationship. I believe my attitude is proper as it is
based on sincere and good friendship with your country which has been
trying to assist independence of Korea.

※ 수신인이 Helmik 소장으로 된 같은 내용의 서한이 있지만 이 자료집에는 싣지 않았다. 이 자료는《민
   세안재홍선집》제2권에 "하지미군사령관에게 보낸 공한 — 민정장관 사의(2차·영문)"란 이름으로 실
   려 있다.

From the international political point of view relationships be-
ween the United States of America, Soviet Russia and North and
South Korean problem, if the American policy toward Korea comes to
the same results as failure, unification of Korea and solution of
current difficult probles in Korea will be delayed, and I waited
patiently.

Now the general election has finished and the national assembly
has opened, and I have definetely decided to be free and want to be
released from my present position.

It might be good in some aspects to hold my position until
completion of transfer of all the executiveworks to the new government, but since I am not able to and not in a position to solve
anything, I do not see any reason t stay any longer.

It has been my hard feeling that I could not solve any problems
by my own power even when I knew the situation very well. I assume
that the new government officials will take care of all the problems
which they are facing.

In the past there were many unfounded criticisms and complaints
in both privated and public affairs, but I know you gentlemen have
confidence in me, and I extend to you respectfully my warm appreciation. There is still some unclered matters, but as far as I am
concerned my conscience is very clear and I am not ashamed of myself.

I would like to add a few words regarding Mr.Kim Koo and Dr. Kim
Kuisic's political north and south joint conference, participated
by many other political leaders. I was in a very difficult position.
However, their intention was not anti-American feelings and pro-
Soviet feelings, because future of Korea manifests that Korean people
cannot be anti-American.

There will be various frictions in the political fields between
Korea and the USA but as one of Korean citizens I sincerely believe
and wish that there will be no change in our mutual and fundamental
confidence in your country which will assist Korea to accomplish her
complete independence.

In fact, it would be very difficult that one country help complete independence of a difference nation, because of historical,
cultural and traditional differences, and conflicting internaational
situation. This point should bever be forgotten by your people and
ours.

In summary, I have accepted the civil administrator's position
sacrififing myself for the purpose of being the first step in the
establishment of unified Korean government, in the time of most
complicated internaational situation,but I regret very much because I
did not accomplish anything. It would be useless for me think over
the past. I shall return to my original faith. Experience of the
past sixteen months does not allow me to participate in government
affairs any longer.

Best wishes to you and good health with great
success.   Yours sincerely,

THE HAN SUNG ILBO
Seoul, Korea

8 June 1948

Lt. Gen. John R. Hodge
Commanding,
Panto Hotel
Seoul, Korea

Dear General,

It is my greatest joy to think that you kindly recall the fact that you were kind enough to make me take over the KEIJO Nippo (Seoul Daily News in Japanese, and organ under Japanese regime) in the forst part of Decmeber, 1945.

Prior to the establishment of the HANSUNG ILBO, THE TONG-A ILBO or the Oriental Daily News moved its office to the KEIJO NIPPO Building.

Under the plea that they greatly cooperated with the past Korean National general election, the leading persons of the Oriental Daily News have been trying to force the Han Sung Ilbo out of the Seoul Kong Insa Building alias the Keijo Nippo building to the effect that the former might monopolize the building. This fact is to be said unlawful. It is true that the HANSUNG ILBO also rendered considerable cooperation to the election, and, if it had been insufficient, the paper as it is has been doing various efforts for the US Military government as well as for Korea. The paper will henceforth render more contribution to them through my personal efforts. I do believe that the HANSUNG ILBO should rather have advantage over the TONG-A ILBO.

It is humbly requested that you kindly take a fair action in consideration with this case.

Doing honour to you,

Respectfully Yours,

AHN CHAI HONG
President

1948年 6月 8日
8 June 1948

Mr. Ahn Chai Hong

Civil Administrator

South Korean Interim Government

Seoul, Korea

南朝鮮過渡政府

民政長官

安在鴻貴下

Dear Mr. Ahn Chai Hong:

貴下의 1948年 6月 1日 付 南朝鮮過渡政府

I am in receipt of your letter dated 1 June 1948 submitting your

民政長官으로서의 辭職願을 接受하였읍니다.

resignation as Civil Administrator of the South Korean Interim Government.

貴下의 書翰은 貴下의 誠意와 所信에 對한

The communication does great credit to the honesty of your convictions

眞實性을 如實히 證明하는것이었읍니다. 本官은

and to your intellectual integrity. It is this great respect for the

貴下의 高貴한 動機에 致賀하며 辭敬하기때문에 躊躇

worthiness of your motives which compels me reluctantly to accept your

하면서 辭職願을 受理하였읍니다. 이 機會에 貴下가

resignation, but I cannot let this occasion pass without expressing my

民政長官職을 通하야 朝鮮國民의 公僕으로서 맡기

deepest appreciation of the services which during your tenure of office

신 貢獻에 對하야 深々한 謝意를 表하지 않을

you have rendered to the Korean people.

수 없읍니다. 南朝鮮過渡政府는 朝鮮民族의

I think history will register as fact that the establishment of

自治政府 樹立에 있어서 가장 重大한 段階이

the South Korean Interim Government was a stage, and a very important

었다는 것은 무론한 事實로 丁史에 남으리라고

stage, on the road to the achievement of self-government by the Korean

Ltr to Mr. Ahn Chai Hong   8 June 1948

민족니다. 軍政은 朝鮮人으로 하여금 現代國家

people. It enabled the Koreans to obtain experience in administration

로서 必要한 行政經驗을 가지도록 하였읍니다. 貴下

of departments which any modern state must possess. You, as Civil

는 民政長官으로서 南朝鮮過渡政府 運營等處

Administrator, played a large part in the conduct and progress of the

에 큰 役割을 하엿읍니다.   貴下는 民政長官으로서

South Korean Interim Government. By your conduct of office and your

忠誠을 다하엿고 最大의 眞摯한 努力을 아끼지 않엇으

loyal, tenacious and sincere efforts, you have left an imprint that

며 그 功績은 歲月이 지남에 따라 더욱 빛나리라고

will grow with the passing years.

민족니다.   貴下의 南朝鮮過渡政府 와 朝鮮民族에

    Would that I could adequately express my appreciation for your

對한 奉仕에 처하여 能히 말도다 謝意를 充分히 表現할수

services to the South Korean Interim Government and the Korean nation.

없음을 遺憾 으로 생각하는同 바에 앞으로 하시는바에도

I wish you the best in your future endeavors, and I know they will be

큰 成功이 있기를 祝願하는 바입니다. 過去에 있어서와 마찬

actuated by the same patriotic and unselfish motives which have led you

가지로 앞으로 무엇을 하시든지 小我를 떠나 眞正한 愛國

in the past as a Korean patriot and statesman.

的 誠意로서 臨하시리라고 確信하는 바입니다.

                        Sincerely,

                        W. F. DEAN

미국육군소장
군 장 장 관
윌. 암. 에푸. 딘

            Major General, United States Army

            Military Governor

181

THE HAŃ SUNG ILBO

12 June 1948

To: Mr. Stewart
    O.C.I.

Dear Sir,

Judging from the history of our establishment following the liberation of 1945, it is not right that the Tong A Ilbo should arbitrarily claim a superior influence for the custody and use of the buildings, machinery and equipments of the Seoul Kong Insa.

I do not want to repeat here the relationship between the Han Sung Ilbo, the Tong A Ilbo and myself following December 1945 as it has been already described in Mr. Kim Chong Ryabg's petition to you. If any superior power is specially to be admitted to the Tong A Ilbo on the ground that it actively supported the general election, then, it must not be overlooked that the Han Sung Ilbo also made certain cooperation with the election, and has contributed greatly to Korea and the US military government in Korea, in its own way.

I myself worked hard as Civil Administrator for the last 16 months and now I am back again to the post of president of the Han Sung Ilbo. I am going to continue my efforts for the great task of establishing the independent Korean government and the unifying north and south Korea.

Now that you have seen our real situation, I firmly believe you have no intention to support the Tong A Ilbo only, disregarding the past relationship of the Han Sung, Tong A and the Soulé Kong Insa, and also our own intention.

I write this letter because when I was going to have a talk with you on the advice of General Dean, I had no chance to do so. If you kindly give me a chance to have a meeting with you, I am sure we can have a very friendly talk.

Respectfully Yours,

President

HEADQUARTERS XXIV CORPS
Office of the Commanding General

APO 235
SEOUL, KOREA

12 June 1948

Mr. Ahn Chai Hong
Civil Administrator
South Korean Interim Government
Seoul, Korea

Dear Mr. Ahn:

I have received your letter of 1 June in which you tender your
resignation as Civil Administrator of the South Korean Interim Government. Your letter is symbolic of the sincerity and moral fortitude
with which you conducted your office. I feel, however, that you have
been unduly critical of your accomplishments. The position which you
held was not one with established precedents, but rather lay in an un-
explored field with its inherent new problems and unclarified policy.
Under such conditions, although certain problems are readily and
skillfully engaged, they are solved only over an extended period of
time, the answer being a summation of individual contributions based
upon a foundation which has been laid with little acclaim.

I believe that as the National Government takes on its administrative responsibilities, it will find both sound precedents and
experienced employees established and trained by you during your tenure.

I accept your resignation reluctantly, feeling that we are losing
a valuable administrator, yet I respect your wishes and appreciate your
desire to engage in a connected although different aspect of service to
your nation.

I wish to express my appreciation for your sincere, loyal work.
I wish you every success in your future endeavor, knowing that it will
be conducted in the true spirit of a Korean patriot and scholar.

Sincerely,

JOHN R. HODGE
Lieutenant General, U. S. Army
Commanding

※ 이 자료는 《민세안재홍선집》 제2권에 "하지사령관의 서한 — 민정장관 사임 수락"이란 이름으로 실려
있다.

南朝鮮過渡政府
民政長官
安在鴻 氏 柄下

一九○八年 二月十三○

民政長官을 辭任하십니다 六月 日字 書翰

抑受하였읍니다 書翰을 書함이 其職責으로

遂行치 誠意외 道德的 勇氣으로 家微하신

그러나 書下을 自己 企業績이 對하여

批判的이라고 本意로 늬기는 바이나 書下

의 書信을 旣定코 失倒가 있었도록가않을인

서로운 問題外 이것 明確되되자않은 政策을

音을 未踏外 分野에 있었도는것이니라 얻어한

問題이 ... 技術的으로 부두처다할지

것을 一로한 時期에 結過하여서 解快되는

여기에서 其解答은 ... 公正도 喝采되이

다른 土台에서라는 個別的이 攻擊이 合計

이것이니다.

本政府가 其目的을 達키爲하여

本官가 駐屯軍과 健全한 前例와 本官가

訓練과 經驗이있는 官吏를 無軍政府를

멸見할것이오며

우리는 本官과 長官은 喪失한다는

咸을깊고 本官은 不得已 本官下의 諸

職을 受諾하노라 一方官은 다므나

圖解된 事業에 本官은 寫하여

從事하게되다는 本官들에 敎育을으~

表하며 咸謝하노라

本官은 本官下의 誠을이있으로 中의업으란 本官

轉에 謝하도表하노라 本官가 以後에도 도움을

한愛名者 學者의 精神으나가 實法을 알므로

本官의 今後 奮鬪에있어서 成功하시기를 바라노라

美軍司令官
죤.알. 하-지中將

KOREAN AFFAIRS INSTITUTE

———————— A NON-PROFIT ORGANIZATION ————————

1029 VERMONT AVE.
NORTHWEST

TELEPHONE
NAtional 7868

"Devoted to Freedom"
WASHINGTON 5, D.C.

June 14, 1948

Mr. An Chaehong
Civil Administrator
South Korea Interim Government
Seoul, Korea

Dear Mr. An:

Although the election in south Korea is over, our nation is facing a grave crisis. As far as the South is concerned, the planning of our national destiny is now entirely in the hands of the Korean leaders. The formation of a government to facilitate our long-desired reunification and our economic rehabilitation has now become the responsibility of the new Assembly.

As you well understand, the Korean nation cannot sustain itself without unity of North and South. You also know that a stable and productive national economy cannot be achieved without the material resources of the North. I am sure you will agree with me that unless economic conditions in south Korea are improved, no government will be able to endure for any length of time. I assume that you are well aware that the trend of the election shows the restlessness of the people. If the new government cannot satisfy the needs and desires of the people, do you not think there would be greater danger of disastrous civil strife within the South itself than of a communist army sweeping down from the North?

No doubt you know that my work here is purely that of disseminating information on developments in Korea, which at times reach important places. Because you are an experienced leader in government affairs, I should like very much to have a statement from you concerning the type of government you wish to have established; how you think the reunification problem should be approached in the immediate future; how the disintegrating economy should be restored to relieve the poverty of the people and the industrial paralysis of the nation; and how outside aid should be solicited and to what extent it is necessary.

A frank statement from you on these subjects will not only satisfy me personally but will be welcomed by many of those who are interested in Korean affairs.

With my best regards,

Sincerely yours,

Yong jeung Kim

YK/dh

P.S. An identical letter is being sent to Mr. Kim Sung Soo of the Hankook Democratic Party.

1948年 6月 22日
22 June 1948

朝鮮 서울

Mr. Ahn, Chai Hong

安 在 鴻 貴下

Seoul, Korea

My dear Mr. Ahn:

貴下가 最近 提出 하신 辭任願의 一
I have received a copy of the letter of resignation which
部를 接受 하였읍니다. 이때에 退任하심에對하
you submitted recently. I regret your leaving at this time but
여 遺憾의 情을 禁치 미려우나 退任의 決意 하신 動機에
I appreciate and respect the reasons you have for making this move.
對하여는 理解하고 敬意를 表하는 바입니다

I wish to express to you my appreciation of the work which
그리고 貴下가 南朝鮮過渡政府를 爲하여 해주
you have done for the South Korean Interim Government. You have
신 그 努力과 業績에 對하여 感謝합니다. 貴下는 政府의
filled a most important post in the Government during unsettled
가장 重大한 職務를 마트섯든것이고 任務完遂를 爲하야
and trying times. You have devoted long hours and great energy to
最大의 努力을 아끼지 않으섯읍니다. 여러가지 難關에 遭着
the task. You have been faced by many obstacles and have worked
하섯스며 그것을 實現하기 爲하여 全力을 다하섯슴니다. 貴下는
hard to overcome them. You have shown great moral and physical
信念과 信念 貫徹을 爲하여는 精神的 及 肉身的 勇氣를 發
courage in carrying out your beliefs and convictions.
揮하섯슴니다. 누구나 目標에 完全히 到達할수는 없읍
None of us ever attains complete success in the objectives
니다. 그러나 貴下로서는 貴下가 自責 하시는 以上의 業績
which we set for ourselves. I believe, however, that you have
을 收기섯읍니다. 때가 지남에 따라서 貴下의 努力
accomplished more than you credit yourself in your letter. As
이 헛되지 않었다는 事實을 充分 認識 하시게 될것
time goes on, you will realize that your time has not been spent
을 確信합니다.
in vain.
官界를 떠나심에 있어서 또 將來하실 事業에 있
In leaving the Government service, you take with you sincere
어서 大成功을 하시기를 心祝하는바밉니다.
wishes for your success in your future undertakings.

Very truly,

C. G. HELMICK
Major General, United States Army
Deputy Military Governor

HEADQUARTERS
UNITED STATES ARMY MILITARY GOVERNMENT IN KOREA
APO 235 Unit 2

12 July 1948

Mr. Ahn, Chai Hong
Chairman, Korean Olympic
   Supporters Association
Seoul, Korea

Dear Mr. Ahn:

     Your letter of July 1st and the very beautiful Olympic handkerchiefs have been received and are very much appreciated. All Americans here in Korea join me in wishing the greatest success to your team. May the Korean Emblem be successful in its contests and in showing to the world the rebirth of the Korean people as a free nation.

     Very sincerely,

     C. G. HELMICK
   Major General, United States Army
    Deputy Military Governor

THE HAN SUNG ILBO
leading Korean press
Seoul, Korea   12 Oct 1948

Mr. J.H.Judd,
Congressman for Minesota,
The House of Representatives,
Washington, D.C.

Dear Mr. Judd,

       Since your departure from Seoul, news about your hard
work in the House of Representatives, which reached me through
the press, have deeply moved my friendly heart. As President
Truman has been reelected, I expect no change will be brought
about in your eastAsian policy, and your Soviet policy with regard to Korean will be friendly and at the same time necessari-
ly firm-handed.

       You will fully recognize that Eastern- problem will never
be solved if China is put under the control of the Communistic
army. At present the Communist army has gained power. They
have temporarily won a victory militarily with the support of
peasants, laborers and petit-boureois at this time when China
is in extreme political disorder and economic disorder, but in
economic construction collapse is bound to take place and there
is no doubt that with your appropriate assistance, democracy
adapted to the present social situation will be reestablished in
China.

       I recognize your active, enlightening and fostering duties
in the congress regarding East Asia and Assistance to China are
tremendously heavy.

       I prey for your health and success.

                       Yours Respectfully,

                            Ahn, Chai Hong
                       (Former Civil Administrator SKIG)

                            President

THE HAN SUNG IL BO
A leading Korean paper
Seoul, Korea

The Honorable Mr. Harry S. Truman,
        President of the United States of America
        Whaite House, Washington, D.C.

                                        12 Oct 1948

My dear Mr. President,

    Your Excellency's reelection to the presidency testifies
to your people's trust in and support to your well-considered
and firm democratic political program. We expect your increas-
ing assistance and support for the achievement of our unified
independence during your coming term of office.

    We believe Your Excellency well recognize the fact that
firm establishment of a democratic government and adjustment
of communistic forces are indispensable conditions for the solution of China problems.

    If Your Excellency succeed in getting Soviet Union's co-
operation for the solution of the difficult problems which have
occurred since the Yalta agreement and for the achievement of
the unified independence of Korea, thus bringing a light of
hope for world peace, Your Excellency will have left an endur-
ing record in the history of mankind.

    I pray for Your Excellency's health and success.

                        Yours Respectfully,

                        Ahn, Chai Hong
                        (Former Civil Administrator SKIG)
                        President

191

NOV 15 1948

Mr. Ahn, Chai Hong
Office of Hansung Ilbo
31-3 Taipyung Ro I Ga
Seoul, Korea

Dear Mr. Ahn:

Acknowledgment is made of the receipt of your letter of 8 November 1948 relative to your plans for the establishment of the "Shin Saing Whae" or "New Life Movement."

Having as it does the altruistic objective of raising the standards of living of the people of Korea it seems to be actuated by the highest of motives. The emphasis on the simple virtues of voluntary industry, thrift and the development of a feeling of brotherhood among men should make a substantial contribution to the life of the people of Korea.

The transfer to the agencies of the Government of Korea of the material items to which you refer has already taken place on a considerable scale and is continuing as more become available.

These goods are turned over to the Provincial Governors and the allocation for distribution and use is made by the Provincial representatives of the Department of Commerce and Industry where, in that Department's opinion, the best interests of the Korean people will be served. It is suggested that you contact this Department relative to the matter.

My best wishes for the success of your movement.

JOHN B. COULTER
Major General, U. S. Army
Commanding

                    THE HAN SUNG ILBO
                    Seoul, Korea

                                            3 Dce 1948

General John R. Hodge,
   Commanding General,
     V Corps, Fort Bragg,
        North Carolina

Dear General,

        I congratulate you on your appointment to the important posi-
tion of commanding general of the V Corps. Your clear-cut and
most appropriate opinion on the Korea problem which is reported
here from time to time makes me to pay great respect to you.

        The rebellions of part of our troops cannot yet be said as
quite settled. Industrial production is becoming shorter due to
shortage of electricity. It is feared that dissatisfaction and
uneasiness of the poeple seem to be considerable.

        If the Chinse communists sweep north China and advance further
toward south, even to threaten Nanking itself, their activities
will seriously affect Korea.   It seems that recently US is losing
her interest in her assistance to China, but, if US should leave
China at the mercy of Chinese communists, you cannot remain optimistic about the fate of Asia, even if US places more stress on
Japan.

        For some time, I am going to keep away from any political
parties which might aim at acquiring political power, and devote
myself to movements for political education of the masses.

        Believing in your unchanged efforts for international demo-
cratic camp and for the democratic independence Republic of Korea,
and wishing you good health and success in the coming New Year.

                            Yours cordially,

                            President

THE HAN SUNG ILBO
Seoul, Korea   3 Dec 1948

Dr. Edgar A.J.Johnson,
    ECA Mission for Korea,
        ECA Building,
    Connecticut Avenue and 'H' Street,
        Washington, D.C.

Dear Dr.,

    It is already over a month since we parted at the wharf of
Inchon. In Korea, the livelihood of the people has become harder
and society unstable due to rebellion of some of our troops under instigation of communists, and to suspension of production
at factories because of shortage in electricity.

    Thoughtful persons are of opinion that much cannot be expect-
ed from the UN General Assembly conferences as it seems that
Korean problem cannot be turned satisfactorily there.

    Continued stay of the US army in Korea is necessary under
the present conditions in Korea. We believe US economic assistance to Korea will be continued as actively as before. We are sure
great effects will be achieved due to your efforts. I recognize
that US has to actively assist Chinese Nationalist Government.
The Chinese problem will, however, determine the destiny of Asia
more in the negative phase.

    I shall be grateful if you will give us some interesting
message through our Han Sung Ilbo. Remember me to Mrs. Johnson
and your son. My wife joins me in my goodwishes to you all. It
is not so easy to get assistance to my New Life Movement from the
US army here. I have met Mr. Goodfellow and have had a good chat
with him.
    Hoping to hear from you soon,

                              Yours cordially,

                              President

1949년

10 January 1949

Ahn, Chai Hong
President, Han Sung Ilbo
Seoul, Korea

Dear Mr. Ahn:

I am extremely grateful for your letter of December 3rd, a letter
that I should have answered long ago, but could not because of the
extreme pressure of work involved in taking over the responsibility
for Korea by ECA.

Your letter was written when there seemed to be some doubt as to
whether the UN General Assembly would approve the recommendations
of UNCOK. Now the situation is greatly changed. I want to congratulate you and the Korean people on the great confidence which
has been reposed in Korea by the General Assembly of the United
Nations.

I appreciate only too well the difficulties with which everyone in
Korea faces. It is only if we work together that we can overcome
these economic adversities. I have learned recently that there is a
movement afoot for consolidating all outstanding political leaders
into one great political movement motivated by genuine patriotism
rather than by political ambitions. I sincerely hope that this
unification movement is going forward because we in America look
upon Korea as the real center of the democratic movement.

Within a day or two I will send you a copy of a talk that I gave to
the Twentieth Century Club in Washington, D.C. If any of this material is useful for publication in the Han Sung Ilbo, you are quite
welcome to reproduce it.

I have not forgotten the matter we discussed at the very pleasant
dinner which Mrs. Johnson and I had with you and Mrs. Ahn. It is
a project that I am trying to explore and I hope that within a
month or six weeks, I may have some news for you. In the meantime,
please convey my very cordial regards to Mrs. Ahn and remember that
you and I have worked long together in a very worthy enterprise.
Please accept, therefore, my very cordial regards and the renewed
assurance of my willing help whenever I can be of service.

Very sincerely yours,

Edgar A. J. Johnson
Director
Korea Division

EAJJ:grm

11 March 1949

Mr. AN, Chai Hong
Editor in Chief
Hansong Ilbo
Seoul, Korea

Dear Mr. An,

Sub-Committee II, which is in charge of the responsibility of studying the question of representative government and its related problems, has instructed me to confirm your appointment for a hearing on Tuesday, 15 March 1949, and the time is 10:30 instead of 10 o'clock, at the Duk Soo Palace.

You will be glad to hear that Dr. M. M. Lee is acting as our interpreter at the hearings.

Members of Sub-Committee I, which is studying the nature of existing barriers between North and South, may be present at the meeting also.

I am enclosing the lists of topics for discussion prepared by both Sub-Committees.

Looking forward to seeing you next Tuesday at 10:30,

Sincerely yours,

Hung-Ti Chu
Secretary
Sub-Committee II

-- 2 --

<u>MAIN TOPICS FOR DISCUSSION AT THE HEARINGS</u> -(Sub-Committee I)

199

(1) What are your views concerning the problem of unification?

(2) What steps, if any, have been taken to promote unification

since the establishment of theGovernment of the Republic

of Korea, and what steps should be taken in this direction?

(3) To what extent is it possible, to remove economic, social

and other barriers in Korea?

A. The development of representative government in Korea

1). Steps taken in the development of representative government
from the establishment of the Republic of Korea to the
present

2). Problems confronting the government and the people in their
efforts for the development of representative government

3). Specific views and proposals on the further development of
representative government

B. The development of representative government in relation to the
problem of unification

1). Political basis for unification

2). Comments on the structure of government and conditions in
North Korea

3). Possibilities of extending representative government within
North Korea

4). Representation and participation of all Koreans in a
unified Korea

第二分科

一. 統一問題에는 口陽援助에依한 軍解決이 最後의機會를 잃지않게하기 為하나 北韓이 百名議會을 選擧케할수있으로 그것對稱、對北의 最善한 工作을 推進할것

二. 民口政府는 統一增進의 積極方針은 아직밝表되어있지... 政府는 口政의 工作을 推進할수있도록 諸... 積極工作을 推進할수있도록

今後 ... 工作의 推進으로 ... 政府의 ... 主義陣營의 聯... 主로 諸國利害에... 軍隊義的 佛을 排他...

二. 今後 一工作이 ... 徒勞에 도라가는限 ... 社會共他의交流로 工業現國難을 ... 工作으로 有無相 通할 ... 要請되는일이다.

A 韓口에서의 代議政治의 發展

一. 口會와 口政首班의 任意 對立抗爭의 激化의 傾向

二. 政府와 ... 一致한 對韓軍事態로 ... 正常한 軌道에 놓

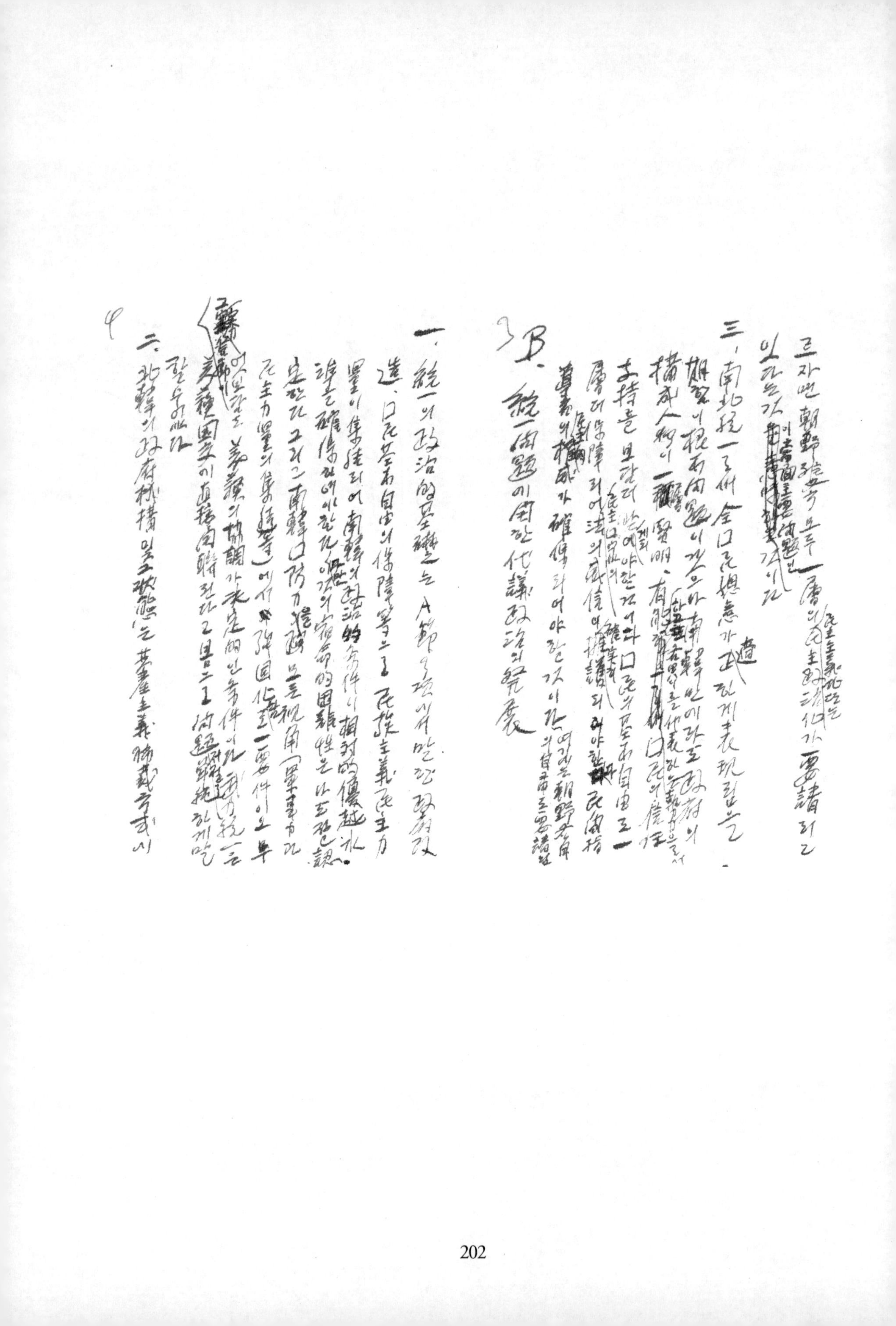

一. 統一의 政治的 基礎는 ⋯

二. 北韓이 ⋯ 政府機構 및 그 狀態는 共産主義 隱蔽武力에 ⋯

三. 南北統一로써 全 口로 民總意가 武力으로 表現되는 ⋯

A.

B. 統一問題에 關한 代議政治의 發展

6

5回

一九四九年三月十五日

吳元世

主要題目 (第一分野)

一、統一問題에 關한 先生님의 高見은 如何하십니까?

二、大韓民國政府 樹立以後 統一을 增進하기 爲하야 었더한 方策을 取하여야 合니까, 이方向에 었더한 方策을 取하야 되겠습니까?

三、어느 程度(範圍)로 韓中에서 經濟 平參 及 其他 이러한 障碍를 除去할수있습니까?

A、

韓國에서의 代議政治의 發展

(第三分集)

一、大韓民子樹立以來 現在까지 代議政治의 發展을 爲한 取한 方策

二、政府와 人民이 代議政治의 發展을 爲한 그비들이 어느方에 있어서 當面問題은

三、代議政治樣去을 發展을 爲한 且傳的 高見을 提議

B、

統一問題에 關한 代議政治의 發展

一、統一의 政治的 基礎

二、北韓의 政府機構及狀態에 關한 高評

三、北韓政에서 代議政治로 延長식이오

四、全韓人이 統一韓國에 代議士로選出及 參加하는件

THE HAN SUNG ILBO
SOUL KOREA

May 6, 1949

Dr. Edgar A J Johnson,
ECA MIssion for Korea
ECA Building, Connecticut Avenue and 'H' Street,
Washington D.C.

Dear Dr. Johnson,
        I thank you very much for your kindness to have given me an
opportunity to see you when you last visited Korea and I am glad
for your assurance that US economic aid policy for our country
is a firm and unchangeable one. But I regret that our two families
could not have a talk together.

        Recently I made a tour of the disturbed areas of Mt. Chiri
and Tukyu of Kyungsang Namdo and Chulla Pukto provinces and made
lectures at seven places for political enlightenment. I am glad
to say that my lectures gave considerable effects in the minds of
the people there.

        I have prepared a booklet of about 110 pages for political
enlightenment of the masses. They will reach the hands of the
citizens by the end of this month.

        I am now writing a second booklet, based on my experience
of my recent lecture tour.

        Whatever may be the circumstances, I shall not cease to work
for our people.

        As for our 'Han Sung Ilbo' we are in the process of organizing
it into a corporation, thus to place it on a firmer financial
basis.

        I am looking forward to seeing you again soon. My wife joins
me in sending regards to Mrs. Johnson and your dear son, and
wishing you a great success.

                    I remain yours cordially,

THE HANSUNG ILBO
Seoul, Korea   8 September 1949

Welcome to US Congressmen!

We wish to express our cordial welcome to Mr. Walter B. Huber and his
party, the distinguished members of the Budget Committee of the House of
Representatives of the US Congress, who are visiting Korea on their tour
of the Far East. The purpose of the tour as we understand it is to obtain
firsthand information of actual conditions prevailing in various countries
in the Far East, so that the US may render more adequate economic assistance
to these countries in building democratic states.

In China, the main-land of Asia, our neibouring country, the communists
are defeating the Nationalists. Korea is a divided country; in the north
there is a force hostile to our democratic development. These factors can
not but cause misgivings to the patriotic-minded elements of our thirty-
million fellow countrymen.

However, by the determined policy of the United States to assist the
Republic of Korea, Koreans have been inspired and encouraged. We believe
that the Republic of Korea will not fail to fulfil the mission of a democratic fortress in the Far East.

The Republic of Korea has ceaselessly struggled for unification and
complete democratic independence in the face of tremendous unfavourable
conditions caused by both international turmoils and internal conflicts.
This fact should not be overlooked nor underestimated.

Although there are conflicting ideas and forces among Koreans, they all
cherish the same desire —Korea must be developed as a free, democratic,
united nation. Many Koreans believe that the emphasis of American policy
has shifted from Asia to Europe. But in terms of population and area, Asia
is more important than Europe.

It goes without saying that any country that controls the Far East
commands the Pacific and, consequently, threatens the United States of
America. The United States of America committed itself to a noble international purpose in the Yalta treaty. It has not completed that mission.
We hope that it will implement the Yalta commitments at the earliest possible
date.

As a means of implementation, President Truman proposed that 150
million dollars be appropriated for economic assistance to Korea. And
the Economic Co-operation Administration proposed that this amount of
assistance be increased. We hope that the Congress will approve the appropriation without any further hesitation. At this juncture, a visit by Congressmen is really significant. We believe that the future of American
assistance to Korea will depend upon you to a great extent. It is encour-
aging to hear that Mr. Huber and his party believe that the Republic of
Korea is a democratic fortress in the Far East; the United States has responsibilities in Korea; the US should continue to assist Korea.

We hope that through the efforts of these distinguished guests Korea
will be better known to the American Congress as well as to the American
people. Once Again we wish to express our welcome and pray for your
health and success.

                                       Civil Administrator
                              President of The Han Sung Ilbo
                              (Former Civil Administrator)

※ 이 자료는 1949년 9월 8일자 한성일보 사설의 영역문이다.

TO THE UN GENERAL ASSEMBLY
(Translation of editorials of the Han Sung Ilbo, 25, 27 Sept 1949)

The Fourth Session of the UN General Assembly has to make proper solution of the Korean problem as well as many other difficult problems. It has to give its best assistance to Korea in her efforts of achieving national unification and democratic national independence so that she may be able to make normal development as a carrier of international-peace.

The Soviet Union with its satellite, Poland, is putting impediment to a fair solution of the Korean problem by refusing to submit it to the General Assembly for consideration. Such an attitude of the Soviet Union will not only impair the international friendship toward the Koreans but also will seriously impede the development of international peace. We cannot but feel great regret. Such an attitude will naturally make the Korean people feel doubt and dissatisfaction toward the Soviet Union.

This makes us feel the more for the urgent necessity of the support and assistance of the UN for the peaceful development of Korea. This is why Korea requested the UN to extend the tenure and power of the UNCOK for the purpose of preventing unexpected disturbances and disasters. The Soviet Union emphatically criticizes American imperialism, but she ought to realize that her own power is giving uneasiness to the Eastern nations.

We know well that United Nations and the USA are not yet tired of assisting Korea to achieve her democratic, national independence. The UN commissions have investigated and studied Korean situation of past and present on the spot for two years and have complied voluminous reports on it. Having such a reliable background about our problems, the UN can be trusted with ease of mind, but we take up the pen again to ask the UN to give our case a deeper reconsideration.

In the past leaders of the Powers have been apt to undervalue the international position of Korea, to overlook the political ability of the Korean people and they seem to know well only the history of misfortunes of the past thousand years as a small and weak nation. But it is mostly overlooked that, on the other hand, her disasterous but independent counter-attacks were not just disasterous. They were not only for self-defence, but also were meritorious in that they secured peace and liberty for her neighbours.

Happening to be situated in the middle of great Powers geopolitically the Koreans have made successive counterattacks for thousands of years. From the 5th century B.C. till the 7th century A.D., there were periodic national wars between China in the west and Korea in the east till Korea was greatly beaten by China in the latter part of the 7th century. Koreans lost greater part of Manchuria but our daring counter-attacks in the southern part of the Korean peninsular successfully broke the invading force of the Chinese and thus prevented them from crossing over to the islands.

Some centuries following the latter part of 10th century was a time when northern tribes or races grew powerful in Mongolia and north Manchuria as Koreans retreated southward, and Koreans had to make a series of daring counterattacks against their disasterous invaders. The most typical counterattacks was the one against the Mongolian invasion of hundred years in the 13th century.

※ 이 자료는 1949년 9월 25, 27일자 한성일보 논설의 영역문이다. 1949년 9월 27일 민세가 부의장으로 참여한 民族陣營强化委員會 제5차 총회는 유엔에 보내는 각서를 채택하여, 30일에 발송하였다.

It was quite clear that, but for the tenacious resistance of the Koreans, Mongolia who had already made complete subjugation of the Chinese mainland and pushed southward as far as the Malayian peninsular, Sumatra and Java, would have trampled upon the Japanese islands. It was over two thousand years ago that the Japanese started their invasion of the Asiatic continent and Korea, being located in the peninsular protruding from the continent, was the first to be attacked. Toward the end of the 16th century, Koreans completely beat back the grand Japanese invasion under Hideyoshi Toyotomi in a war of seven years.

China of Ming Dynasity sent her troops all the time to assist Korea. True it is that China ought to be thanked for her assistance, but the merits of the seven years' resistance of Koreans, which stopped Japanese invasion of China for three and half centuries, ought to be valued higher. We seldom find a nation who correctly realize the great international merits of the Korean people who made lasting contributions not only for her own independence but also for the freedom and security of all the Oriental nations. We warn that the US, United Kingdom, China, Soviet Union, France and other world Powers should deeply realize this fact anew.

The resolution of the Second Session of the UN General Assembly of Nov 14, 1947 to establish a unified, democratic government in Korea through a general election throughout the land under the observation of the UNTCOK was the last chance of peaceful solution of the Korean problem with international assistance, but the task was not accomplished due to non-cooperation of the Soviet Union. The Republic of Korea was establis hed but its rule does not extend to north of the 38th Parallel and it is facing many bad conditions. The origin of all this stems from the Soviet non-cooperation.

This year, the Fourth General Assembly is being held and Korean problem has been decided to be handled before everthing else. This indicates that international morality is still alive.

At the Third General Assembly of Dec 12, 1948 forty-eight nations voted for the support and recognition of the Republic of Korea. Since then altogether 22 nations including Iran individually accorded recognition to the Republic. It is requested that world democratic nations should secure Korea as a peace base of the Asiatic continent and a stronghold of democracy by their unchanging joint policy toward Korea.

It is also hoped that the Soviet Union will discard her mistaken policy and adopt a completely new policy considering the true will of the greatest number of the thirty-million Koreans, so that as not to impede the great task of national unification of Korea.

In the 7th century the Chinese made 12 great invasions of Korea for 70 years till Korea became a weak nation. The only thing gained by China was merely to open a gate of escape for periodic invasion of China by the most cruel northern tribes and races. As a result China became to share the destiny of certain resistance with the Koreans.

The correct words of Generalissimo Chang Kae-shek that 'There is no true independence of China without complete independence of Korea' is a repentence, as the conclusion of the historical settlement of accounts of over twelve hundred years since the 7th century.

Kitai, Mongols and other tribes and races, who had risen in the north since the 10th century, without exception, invaded Korea and China and their business was to commit atrocious deeds. But, while the Koreans and the Chinese still exist, nothing remains of the northern invaders except vestages of murders and plunders. It is too clear that they made no contributions to human culture.

The Japanese in modern times prospered for some decades by invading northward, but it only proved to be the cause of her unprecidented defeat. The prosperity and glory of a generation became no more than a national nightmare.

Though Korea had become a weak nation, her neighbouring nations could not subjugate her at last. It has been proved by history that power can make a temporary conquest but fails in the end. The Soviet Union should realize this historical fact and the US and united nations too understand it anew. Atomic bombs have been discovered, but no nation can dare to boast of masses slaughter.

Since the announcement of three principles of American policy toward China by John Hay in 1900, the US and China have been traditionally the greatest friendly nations for half a century. But american assistance toward China ceased with the mediation of General Marshall for the Kwomingtang-Communist rapproachment.

There is a great difference between Korea and China with respect to area, population, productions and consumption, but there can be no security of China and the entire East without peace of Korea. Therefore, it is not sound to make any hasty decision as to the relative gravity of Korea and China with respect to international security and peace. The value of Korea as a democratic stronghold has greatly increased because of the loss of influence of the Chinse nationalist government.

Some may think that Japanese ability is worth using, but Japanese islands are away from the continent. It is all right to allow the Japanese to rise up again as a democratic and peaceful nation, but they should by all means be prevented from doing the same things on either shore of the Pacific as the Germans did in 1932.

As regards the relations with the Soviet Union, Turkey in west and Korea in the east of the Soviet Union are in a similar position in that both countries are in the way of Russian southward movement. Those who dominate the Korean peninsular will surely dominate the whole East and the Pacific. The reason why Korean problem should not be undervalued is quite clear. It is good both for the USA and Soviet Russia and for the stability of international influences, to help Korea to accomplish her democratic independence in her fatherland, so that she can be the pillar of peace. Statesmen of the United Nations and the USA should continue their unchanged support of Korea. International feeling of love and hate is not a thing fixed but one which fluctuates according to the mutual relationship. To emphasize this point is our desire for a true friendly relationship with the Soviet Union.

The End

United States Senate

COMMITTEE ON FOREIGN RELATIONS

October 14, 1949.

Mr. Ahn Chai Hong
President,
The Han Sung Ilbo,
Seoul, Korea.

Dear Sir :

This will acknowledge your note of September 30th which has just received. With the copy of a translations of certain editorials on the Korean problem, it will be brought to the attention of Chairman Connally.

Very truly yours,

C. C. O'Day

Clerk- Committee on Foreign
Relations.

※ 이 자료는 208쪽 "UN 총회에 보내는 글"에 대한 답신이다.

1965년

■ **사진_** 1965년 3월 9일 민세 추도식. 인사말을 하고 있는 이인(당시 대법원장) 장례위원장.

UNITED NATIONS COMMAND
OFFICE OF THE COMMANDER IN CHIEF
APO SAN FRANCISCO 96301

19 March 1965

Dear Mrs. Kim and Mr. Ahn:

I am in receipt of your letter, dated 3 March 1965, relative to your request that the United Nations Command Component, Military Armistice Commission, assist you in obtaining the remains of your late husband and father.

The Military Armistice Commission is required to restrict its activities to supervising and implementing the provisions of the Military Armistice Agreement. In view of this, it is regretted that this command is not able to assist you in this matter. However, in an attempt to provide whatever assistance may be possible, I have forwarded your letter to the Republic of Korea Government for any action that it may deem appropriate.

Sincerely,

HAMILTON H. HOWZE
General, United States Army
Commander in Chief

Mrs. Boo Ray Kim
Mr. Jung Yong Ahn
Petitioners
San 11-152 Donam Dong,
Sungbook Ku
Seoul, Korea

215

국제 연합군 사령부
군우 301

1965년 3월 19일

한국 서울 성북구 돈암동 산 11의 152
진정인: 김 부래 여사 및 안 정용 씨 귀하

친애하는 김 여사 및 안 씨:

군사 정전 위원회 국제 연합군측 성원이 여러분으로 하여금 여러분의 부군 되시고 선친되시는 고인의 유해를 입수하는 데 도와 주도록 여러분이 요청하는 1965년 3월 3일부 여러분의 서신을 본인은 접수했읍니다.

군사 정전 위원회의 활동은 군사 정전 협정상의 제반 조항을 감독하며 실시 하는 데 국한시키도록 요구되고 있읍니다. 이 점에 비추어 본 사령부가 이 문제에 있어 여러분을 도와드리지 못함을 유감으로 여기는 바입니다. 그러나 가능한 여지 가 있는 무슨 도움이라도 제공해 드리려는 생각에서 본인은 대한민국 정부가 적절 하다고 사료하는 어떠한 조치든지 취할 수 있도록 여러분의 서신을 당해 정부에 전달하였읍니다.

사령관
미 합중국 육군 대장
해밀튼 에이취. 하우즈

연대 미상

■ **사진_** 연대 미상. 38선 경비대 순시 차 여현(礪峴)을 찾은 민세.

魏德邁

Fort Meade, Md.

Dear Mrs Ahn,

How lovely of you to send me that beautiful piece of yellow jade! It is truly magnificent and I appreciate it more than I can ever tell you.

Al has spoken of you to me, and told me how kind you were to him. I hope so much that some day I will have the pleasure

※ Dade Wedemeyer는 A. C. Wedemeyer 중장의 부인으로, Wedemeyer 중장은 1946년 3월(주중 미군 사령관)과 1947년 7월(대통령 특사)에 두 차례 방한하였다.

of meeting you, and thank-
ing you in person.

He joins me in sending
heart-felt good wishes to
your fine country and yourself.

Sincerely and gratefully,
Dade Wedemeyer

September twenty-second

TO: AHN JAI HONG
CIVIL ADMINISTRATOR

民政長官　安在鴻氏　閣下

Mr. Ahn Chai Hong:

　　本官이 듯기에는　田耕武
I am told that Jacob

　　氏屍体가　田 飛行機로서
Dunns body will be placed

火曜日(来由)　午后 五時에 日本을
on a plane leaving Japan

出發하여 朝鮮으로 오리라 합니다.
at 5:00 Pm Tuesday for

　　또 듯건대　運賃은
Korea. Also that no

걸리지 않한다 합니다.
expense will be involved.

ARCHER L. LERCH
美國　陸軍少將
Major General, United States Army
顧問官
ADVISER
南朝鮮過渡政府
SOUTH KOREA INTERIM GOVERNMENT

※ 조선체육회 부회장 전경무는 1946년 8월 31일 제14회 올림픽 참가교섭을 위해 도미하였고, 1947년 6월 국제올림픽위원회 조선대표로 참석차 스톡홀름으로 가던 중 비행기 사고로 사망하였다.

May 23.

Dear Mr. Ahn,

I trust that you are enjoying your work and are producing fine results.

It is gratifying to have the Joint Commission at work again. I am sure that the required results will be obtained if the Koreans will present a united front in support of the U. S. effort.

I have sent a copy of the enclosed editorial to Dr. Rhee in the hope that he may lead the Korean people in the proper path.

Sincerely

A V Arnold
Maj Gen USA.

※ Arnold 소장은 1945년 9월 12일에 군정장관으로 임명되었고, 1946년 1월 8일 A. L. Lerch 소장으로 교체되었다.

Mr. Ahn Chai Hong
Civil Administrator
Military Government.

General Hodge, and ladies and gentlemen,

The great task of aiding Korea in founding an independent country for the sake of the Korean people is being world-widly observed with keen interests.

Not only is the completion of this great task a great event in the history of the Korean independanee , but also it will be recorded on the history of the owrld with great brilliancy. This great work must be accomplished by any means.

To accomplish this historical work not only all the Koreans are requried to cooperate with Military Government of the United States of America in Korea from the standpoint of accomplishment of the independence of Korea, but also all the Direcoers and the other personnel of the Government ought to cooperate with the Administration of the United States of America with the spirit of the patriots for the independence of Korea.

The business of the Military Governmr who finally decides and leads the great work has a close concern with the preeeding efforts rendered by the Koreas and the Korean government personnel under Military administration.

Now, the appointed Military Governor Maj. General William F. Dean is a very able Army general in the United States Army. General Dean has rendered brilliant service in the great landing operation in France at Normandie. I,therefore, do believe that he with such good judgement and firm resolution will achieve the great task of aiding Korea in granting the independence of Korea. It is very difficult work for the peoples who have different history and tradition from each other to push the great task of the foundation of Korea.

It can never be a simple problem. Our task which is restricted by the complicated international relations is not easy. Therefore, we feel more and more the necessity of such an able, intelligent amn as General Dean. The more we feel this necessity, the more warmly we welcome him and congratulate him on the appointment.

AHN CHAI HONG
Civil Administrator

※ W. F. Dean 소장은 1947년 10월 30일에 군정장관으로 임명되었다.